W9-AXI-424

Air Pollution

Other Books of Related Interest:

At Issue Series

The Energy Crisis

Should the U.S. Reduce Its Consumption?

Wave and Tidal Power

Current Controversies Series

Conserving the Environment

The Green Movement

Nuclear Energy

Oil

Vegetarianism

Global Viewpoints Series

Garbage and Recycling

Oil

Population Growth

Introducing Issues with Opposing Viewpoints Series

Organic Food and Farming

Issues That Concern You Series

Alternative Energy

Going Green

Pollution

Opposing Viewpoints Series

China

Energy Alternatives

Air Pollution

Margaret Haerens, Book Editor

GREENHAVEN PRESS
A part of Gale, Cengage Learning

GALE
CENGAGE Learning

Detroit • New York • San Francisco • New Haven, Conn • Waterville, Maine • London

Christine Nasso, *Publisher*
Elizabeth Des Chenes, *Managing Editor*

© 2011 Greenhaven Press, a part of Gale, Cengage Learning

Gale and Greenhaven Press are registered trademarks used herein under license.

For more information, contact:
Greenhaven Press
27500 Drake Rd.
Farmington Hills, MI 48331-3535
Or you can visit our Internet site at gale.cengage.com

For product information and technology assistance, contact us at

Gale Customer Support, 1-800-877-4253
For permission to use material from this text or product, submit all requests online at www.cengage.com/permissions

Further permissions questions can be emailed to permissionrequest@cengage.com

Articles in Greenhaven Press anthologies are often edited for length to meet page require-ments. In addition, original titles of these works are changed to clearly present the main thesis and to explicitly indicate the author's opinion. Every effort is made to ensure that Greenhaven Press accurately reflects the original intent of the authors. Every effort has been made to trace the owners of copyrighted material.

Cover image © Dennis Cox/Alamy.

LIBRARY OF CONGRESS CATALOGING-IN-PUBLICATION DATA

Air pollution / Margaret Haerens, book editor.
        p. cm. -- (Global viewpoints)
    Includes bibliographical references and index.
    ISBN 978-0-7377-5185-7 (hardcover) -- ISBN 978-0-7377-5186-4 (pbk.)
    1. Air pollution. I. Haerens, Margaret.
    TD883.A47133 2011
    363.739'2--dc22
                                                    2010040831

Printed in the United States of America
1 2 3 4 5 6 7 15 14 13 12 11

Contents

Chapter 2: The Health Effects of Air Pollution

Chapter 3: The Political and Economical Effects of Air Pollution Policy

Chapter 4: Strategies for Reducing Air Pollution

Foreword

> "The problems of all of humanity can only be solved by all of humanity."
> —Swiss author Friedrich Dürrenmatt

Global interdependence has become an undeniable reality. Mass media and technology have increased worldwide access to information and created a society of global citizens. Understanding and navigating this global community is a challenge, requiring a high degree of information literacy and a new level of learning sophistication.

Building on the success of its flagship series, *Opposing Viewpoints*, Greenhaven Press has created the *Global Viewpoints* series to examine a broad range of current, often controversial topics of worldwide importance from a variety of international perspectives. Providing students and other readers with the information they need to explore global connections and think critically about worldwide implications, each *Global Viewpoints* volume offers a panoramic view of a topic of widespread significance.

Drugs, famine, immigration—a broad, international treatment is essential to do justice to social, environmental, health, and political issues such as these. Junior high, high school, and early college students, as well as general readers, can all use *Global Viewpoints* anthologies to discern the complexities relating to each issue. Readers will be able to examine unique national perspectives while, at the same time, appreciating the interconnectedness that global priorities bring to all nations and cultures.

Material in each volume is selected from a diverse range of sources, including journals, magazines, newspapers, nonfiction books, speeches, government documents, pamphlets, organization newsletters, and position papers. *Global Viewpoints* is truly global, with material drawn primarily from international sources available in English and secondarily from U.S. sources with extensive international coverage.

Features of each volume in the *Global Viewpoints* series include:

- An **annotated table of contents** that provides a brief summary of each essay in the volume, including the name of the country or area covered in the essay.

- An **introduction** specific to the volume topic.

- A **world map** to help readers locate the countries or areas covered in the essays.

- For each viewpoint, an **introduction** that contains notes about the author and source of the viewpoint explains why material from the specific country is being presented, summarizes the main points of the viewpoint, and offers three **guided reading questions** to aid in understanding and comprehension.

- **For further discussion** questions that promote critical thinking by asking the reader to compare and contrast aspects of the viewpoints or draw conclusions about perspectives and arguments.

- A worldwide list of **organizations to contact** for readers seeking additional information.

- A **periodical bibliography** for each chapter and a **bibliography of books** on the volume topic to aid in further research.

- A comprehensive **subject index** to offer access to people, places, events, and subjects cited in the text, with the countries covered in the viewpoints highlighted.

Global Viewpoints is designed for a broad spectrum of readers who want to learn more about current events, history, political science, government, international relations, economics, environmental science, world cultures, and sociology— students doing research for class assignments or debates, teachers and faculty seeking to supplement course materials, and others wanting to understand current issues better. By presenting how people in various countries perceive the root causes, current consequences, and proposed solutions to worldwide challenges, *Global Viewpoints* volumes offer readers opportunities to enhance their global awareness and their knowledge of cultures worldwide.

Introduction

"The health effects of air pollution imperil human lives. This fact is well documented."

—Congresswoman
Eddie Bernice Johnson,
Motion to Instruct Conferees on
H.R. 6, Energy Policy Act of 2003,
October 29, 2003

Air pollution remains a serious worldwide threat to the health of humans, animals, and vegetation. Despite attempts to alleviate the problem through environmental regulations and policies as well as advancement in technology, man-made pollution continues to permeate the air in industrialized areas and results in health problems such as asthma, cancer, and emphysema. According to a majority of climate scientists, it also contributes to global climate change. As carbon dioxide and other air pollution collects in the atmosphere, it acts like a blanket, trapping the sun's heat and causing higher temperatures. As politicians and environmentalists struggle with efficacious ways to address the hazards of man-made pollution, incidents in China and Russia in 2010 had devastating health and economic consequences and intensified the debate over greenhouse gas emissions (natural and man-made gas that traps heat in the atmosphere) and global climate change.

In March 2010 a destructive sandstorm blanketed sixteen provinces across western and central China, including the capital city of Beijing, and reached areas as far away as Hong Kong and Taiwan. Although Chinese sandstorms are not uncommon, the Chinese Academy of Sciences estimates that the frequency has risen sixfold in the past fifty years to about two dozen a year. The ferocity of the March 2010 sandstorm was very unusual. Originating in the Gobi Desert, which is the largest desert in Asia, winds swept across the desert sands and mixed with industrial pollution already in the air to create blinding, suffocating sandstorms.

According to the China Meteorological Administration, more than a quarter of China is covered in sand, with desertification threatening to swallow more of China's land. The problem has been aggravated by deforestation, overpopulation, urban sprawl, and overgrazing of livestock. Climate change is also thought to play a central role in the encroaching desertification that has environmentalists alarmed.

The health and economic impact of the March 2010 sandstorms was immense. People who breathed in the sand, grit, and industrial pollution from the whirling sandstorms experienced chest discomfort and respiratory problems. The elements contained in the sandstorm also got into machines, causing malfunctions or complete breakdowns. Numerous airline flights were cancelled and other transportation was postponed. Millions of animals, including valuable livestock, were killed and crops were ruined by a thick, suffocating layer of sand. In Beijing, the air quality was measured at level five at the height of the sandstorm, and record levels of air pollution were measured in Hong Kong.

Another natural disaster in 2010 illuminated the considerable health and economic consequences of air pollution. In July of that year, a series of wildfires broke out across Russia, concentrated mainly in the western part of the country. Hundreds of devastating fires were attributed to unprecedented high temperatures—the summer of 2010 was the hottest summer in Russia in 130 years of record keeping—and crippling drought in the region. As a result of the extensive fires, one-third of the nation's wheat crop was destroyed, leading the Russian government to ban wheat exports through the end of the year and sending world grain prices to new highs. More than fifty people were killed, along with countless animals. Houses were obliterated by the fast-moving flames, leaving more than three thousand people homeless. A thick, acrid smoke blanketed Moscow, a city of ten million people, forcing citizens to don masks and stay indoors. The dry peat bogs (deposits of partially decayed vegetation matter that can be used for fuel) east of the city exacerbated the air pollution, releasing large amounts of carbon dioxide into the smoky Moscow air. The levels of air pollution in Russia's capital city jumped to very dangerous levels. Most worrisome, however, was that at one point the wide-ranging fires threatened to engulf areas contaminated by the Chernobyl nuclear accident, which could have resulted in the spread of radioactive smoke.

The impact of these two disasters was incalculable—not just the short-term economic costs of lost crops, ruined equipment, or canceled airline flights, but the long-term cost of health problems, like asthma or lung cancer, and environmental damage to land coated by sand and grit or destroyed by fire. It will take years for the true cost of these damaging events to become clear.

There are political implications, too. The Chinese sandstorms and Russian wildfires also reignited the debate over global climate change in countries that have been criticized for their treatment of the issue in the past. In China, experts noted that the desertification of China has been accelerated by deforestation, the spread of agriculture, urban sprawl, and overpopulation. The severe droughts in many regions that exacerbate the process of desertification, argue many scientists, can be directly attributed to the impact of climate change. One step the Chinese government has taken is to plant billions of trees to offset greenhouse gas emissions, a process called reforestation. According to Karen Bennett of the World Resources Institute (WRI) in an August 5, 2008, article posted on the WRI website, "Since 2001, [China has] spent nearly $9 billion trying to restore ecosystem services by planting forests, establishing desert vegetation and creating a 330-[kilometer] belt of trees to manage the advancing desert."

In the case of the Russian wildfires, environmentalists maintain that the unprecedented high temperatures that are blamed for the fires can be viewed as a deadly effect of global climate change, particularly the steady increase of greenhouse gas concentrations in Russia. According to Alexei Kokorin, head of the climate and energy program at World Wildlife Fund (WWF) Russia, until the government addresses greenhouse gas emission, the problem of wildfires will continue to be a threat. "We have to get ready to fight such fires in the future because there is a great possibility that such a summer will be repeated," he contends in an August 10, 2010, BBC report. "This tendency won't stop in the coming 40 years or so, until the greenhouse gas emissions are reduced."

The authors of the viewpoints presented in *Global Viewpoints: Air Pollution* discuss some of the key issues of global concern, including the state of air quality worldwide, the health effects of air pollution, the political and economical impacts of air pollution, and new and evolving strategies to address the dangerous problem of air pollution. The information contained in this volume provides insight into the recurring conflict between environmentalists who want to put into place policies and regulations to improve air quality and governments and businesses that want to balance that with economic growth and development. The viewpoints in this book also explore different types of air pollution and air quality issues relevant not only to a specific region, community, or class, but also of global concern to all countries—developed or developing.

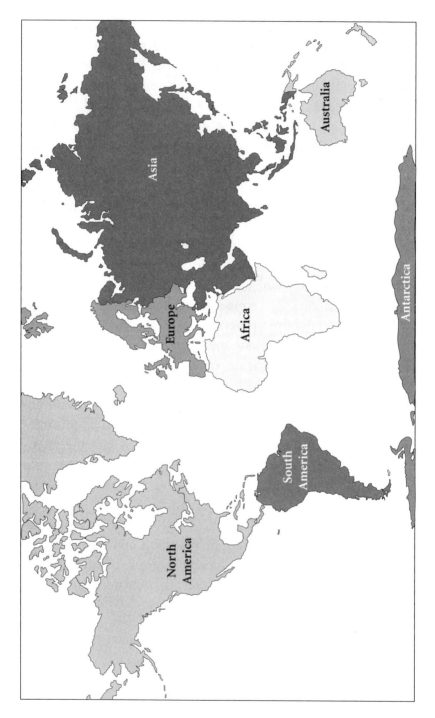

GLOBALVIEWPOINTS

CHAPTER 1

| Air Quality Worldwide

The Global Air Quality Outlook: An Overview

United Nations Environment Programme

The United Nations Environment Programme (UNEP) is the designated United Nations organization that coordinates environmental policy and activity. In the following viewpoint, UNEP details the devastating effect air pollution has on human health, agriculture, forest growth, animal life, and ecosystem health. It also contends that global attempts to manage air pollution have met with mixed results.

As you read, consider the following questions:

1. According to the World Health Organization, how many people die from fine particle pollution every year?
2. What nations are estimated to suffer about two-thirds of the world's premature deaths due to indoor and outdoor air pollution?
3. How many people die prematurely each year from exposure to polluted indoor air?

Human and environmental exposure to air pollution is a major challenge, and an issue of global concern for public health. The World Health Organization (WHO) estimated that about 2.4 million people die prematurely every year due to fine particles. This includes about 800,000 deaths due to outdoor urban PM_{10} [coarse and fine particulates], and 1.6 million due to indoor PM_{10}, even though the study did not include all mortality causes likely to be related to air pollution. . . . The highest number of estimated annual premature deaths occurs in developing countries of Asia and the Pacific.

Besides effects on human health, air pollution has adverse impacts on crop yields, forest growth, ecosystem structure and function, materials and visibility. Once released into the atmosphere, air pollutants can be carried by winds, mix with other pollutants, undergo chemical transformations and eventually be deposited on various surfaces.

Atmospheric Emissions and Air Pollution Trends

Emissions in the various regions show different trends for SO_2 [sulphur dioxide] and NO_x [nitrous oxide]. There have been decreases in the national emissions in the more affluent countries of Europe and North America since 1987. More recently Europe is as concerned with unregulated sulphur emissions from international shipping as it is with the regulated land-based sources. For the industrializing nations of Asia, emissions have increased, sometimes dramatically, over the last two decades. There are no aggregate data for regions after 2000, and therefore recent changes in emissions of developing countries are not displayed, especially in Asia. For instance, from 2000 to 2005 the Chinese SO_2 emissions increased by approximately 28 per cent, and satellite data suggest that NO_x emissions in China have grown by 50 per cent between 1996 and 2003. The main result is that global emissions of SO_2 and NO_x are increasing with respect to 1990 levels. In Africa, and in Latin America and the Caribbean, small increases have been reported.

In many large cities in developing countries, current air pollution concentrations are very high, especially for PM_{10}. However, pollutant levels are decreasing, usually because of controls on emission sources, changing fuel use patterns, and closures of obsolete industrial facilities. For lead, the trends are decreasing, and ambient levels in most cities are currently below the WHO guideline. In general, PM_{10} and SO_2 levels have been decreasing, although levels of PM_{10} are still many times higher than the WHO guideline in many developing countries, and SO_2 levels are above the WHO guideline in a number of cities and differences are considerable in different regions. Most large cities exceed the WHO guideline for NO_2 [nitrogen dioxide], and the levels are not showing any significant decreases.

Modelling indicates the highest levels of tropospheric ozone—a major component of photochemical smog—are in a subtropical belt that includes southeastern parts of North America, southern Europe, northern Africa, the Arabian Peninsula, and the southern and northeastern parts of Asia. However, there is currently a lack of rural measurements in Asia, Africa and Latin America that could validate these results. There is a trend of rising annual mean tropospheric ozone concentrations across the northern hemisphere that implies that several regions may need to cooperate to address the problem.

In addition, clouds of tiny aerosol particles from emissions hang over a number of regions (known as atmospheric brown clouds). These seasonal layers of haze reduce the amount of sunlight that can reach the earth's surface, which has potential direct and indirect impacts on the water cycle, agriculture and human health. The aerosols and other particulate air pollutants in the atmosphere absorb solar energy and reflect sunlight back into space.

Features of Different Air Pollutants

Six common pollutants—suspended particulate matter (SPM), sulphur dioxide (SO_2), nitrogen dioxide (NO_2), carbon monoxide (CO), tropospheric ozone (O_3) and lead (Pb)—harm human health, and are used as indicators of air quality by regulatory agencies.... PM [particulate matter] is distinguished as different inhalable fractions that are classified as coarse and fine particulates with aerodynamic diameters below 10 μm (PM_{10}) and 2.5 μm ($PM_{2.5}$) respectively.

Air pollutants may be considered primary—entitled directly into the air—or secondary pollutants that are formed in the air by chemical and/or photochemical reactions on primary pollutants. The formation of secondary pollutants, such as tropospheric ozone and secondary aerosols, ... is strongly dependent on climate and atmospheric composition. Due to atmospheric transport, their impacts can occur far from their sources.

The major chemical components of PM are sulphate, nitrate, ammonium, organic carbon, elemental carbon and soil dust (consisting of several mineral elements). Other important primary pollutants include heavy metals, such as mercury, cadmium and arsenic; VOCs, such as benzene, toluene, ethylbenzene and xylenes; polycyclic aromatic hydrocarbons (PAHs); and some persistent organic pollutants (POPs), such as dioxins and furans. These air pollutants result from the burning of fossil fuels, biomass and solid waste. Ammonia (NH_3) is emitted primarily from agricultural sources.

United Nations Environment Programme,
Global Environmental Outlook 4, *2007. www.unep.org.*

Effects of Air Pollution

Air pollution is one of the major environmental factors causing adverse impacts on human health, crops, ecosystems and
materials, with priorities varying among regions. Both indoor
and outdoor air pollution are associated with a broad range of
acute and chronic impacts on health, with the specific type of
the impact depending on the characteristics of the pollutant.
The developing nations of northeast, southeast and southern
Asia are estimated to suffer about two-thirds of the world's
premature deaths due to indoor and outdoor air pollution.

The most important air pollutant from a disease perspective is fine particulate matter. WHO estimated that particulates in urban areas worldwide cause about 2 per cent of mortality from cardiopulmonary disease in adults, 5 per cent of
mortality from cancers of the trachea, bronchus and lung, and
about 1 per cent of mortality from acute respiratory infections in children, amounting to about 1 per cent of premature
deaths in the world each year. In addition, the WHO estimated that indoor smoke from solid fuel causes about one-
third of lower respiratory infections, about one-fifth of chronic
obstructive pulmonary disease, and approximately 1 per cent
of cancers at the trachea, bronchus and lung. . . .

*Both indoor and outdoor air pollution are associated
with a broad range of acute and chronic impacts on
health, with the specific type of the impact depending on
the characteristics of the pollutant.*

The health impacts of air pollution are closely linked with
poverty and gender issues. Women in poor families bear a dis-
proportionate burden of the impacts of air pollution due to
their greater exposure to smoke from poor-quality fuel for
cooking. In general, the poor are more exposed to air pollu-

tion due to the location of their residences and workplaces, and their increased susceptibility due to such factors as poor nutrition and medical care.

Impact on Agriculture

Air pollution also adversely affects agriculture. Measurable, regional-scale impacts on crop yields caused by tropospheric ozone have been estimated to cause economic losses for 23 arable crops in Europe in the range US$5.72–12 billion/year. There is evidence of significant adverse effects on staple crops in some developing countries, such as India, Pakistan and China, which are now starting to deal with this issue.

In 1987 the regional impacts of acid rain caused by sulphur and nitrogen deposition were of major importance in Europe and North America, causing lake acidification and forest decline, mainly due to soil acidification. More recently, such declines have also been documented in Mexico and China, and are probably occurring in many other countries. There is recent evidence that emission controls led to a reversal of freshwater acidification, and the dire warnings related to widespread forest decline across Europe and North America at the time of the Brundtland Commission have not materialized. There is now a risk of acidification in other areas of the world, particularly Asia.

Other Damage

Over recent decades the eutrophying effect of nitrogen deposition has also caused significant loss of biodiversity in some sensitive, nutrient-limited ecosystems, such as heaths, bogs and mires in northern Europe and North America. Nitrogen deposition has been recognized within the Convention on Biological Diversity as a significant driver of species loss. Several major global biodiversity hot spots have been identified as being at significant risk because of nitrogen deposition.

The built environment is affected by air pollution in several ways. Soot particles and dust from transport are deposited on monuments and buildings, SO_2 and acid deposition induces corrosion of stone and metal structures and ozone attacks many synthetic materials, decreasing their useful life, and degrading their appearance. All these effects impose significant costs for maintenance and replacement. In addition, fine particles in urban environments typically reduce visibility by one order of magnitude.

Persistent organic pollutants (POPs) and mercury have emerged as important issues since 1987. These toxic substances become volatile when emitted to the environment, and can then be transported over long distances. When pollutants are persistent, concentrations will build up in the environment, causing a risk of bioaccumulation in food chains. Many POPs are now found around the globe, even far from their sources. In the Arctic environment, harmful health effects have been observed in northern wildlife, and the pollution threatens the integrity of traditional food systems and the health of indigenous peoples.

The considerable progress that has been made in preventing and controlling air pollution in many parts of the world has been achieved largely through command-and-control measures, both at the national and regional levels.

Managing Air Pollution

Progress in managing air pollution presents a mixed picture. Urban air pollution remains a critical issue, affecting people's health in many developing countries, although progress is evident in high-income countries. Some regional air pollution issues, such as acid rain, have been successfully addressed in Europe, but they pose a threat in parts of Asia. Tropospheric ozone has emerged as a particularly intractable problem, mainly in the northern hemisphere, where it affects crops and health. Burning biomass fuels indoors in developing regions imposes an enormous health burden on poor families, especially women and young children. Action in developing countries has been inadequate to date, but there remains an opportunity to improve health and reduce premature mortality.

The considerable progress that has been made in preventing and controlling air pollution in many parts of the world has been achieved largely through command-and-control measures, both at the national and regional levels. At the national level, many countries have clean air legislation that sets emission and ambient air quality standards to protect public health and the environment. At the regional level, examples include the Convention on Long-Range Transboundary Air Pollution, the Canada-U.S. Air Quality Agreement and European Union legislation. Other emerging regional intergovernmental agreements include the ASEAN [Association of Southeast Asian Nations] Haze Agreement, the Malé Declaration on the Control and Prevention of Air Pollution in South Asia, and the Air Pollution Information Network for Africa, a regional science-policy network. At the global level, the Stockholm Convention on Persistent Organic Pollutants regulates the use and emission of certain pollutants (POPs). Although the Brundtland Commission highlighted the issue of mercury in the environment, no global agreement to limit mercury contamination has been reached. There has been a global mercury programme operational since 2001, and changes in technology and the use of alternative compounds seem to have reduced emissions.

Transport Emissions

Fuel and vehicle technologies have improved substantially during the last two decades, driven both by technological and legislative developments. Vehicle emissions have been partially controlled by the removal of lead from gasoline, requirements for catalytic converters, improved evaporative emission controls, fuel improvements, on-board diagnostic systems and other measures. Diesel vehicle emissions have been reduced by improved engine design and, for some vehicles, particle traps. Widespread use of particle traps will await reductions of sulphur in diesel fuel to below 15 ppm [parts per million]. Current diesel fuel sulphur levels differ considerably among regions. Reducing sulphur in gasoline to low levels enables use of more effective catalytic converters, thus leading to improved emission control. Hybrid gasoline electric vehicles, which tend to be more fuel efficient in urban traffic than gasoline-only vehicles, have been introduced in many developed countries, but their use is still very limited.

Most developed countries have made substantial progress in reducing per vehicle emissions, and many middle-income countries have implemented significant measures to control vehicle emissions. In addition to improved vehicle technologies, effective vehicle inspection and maintenance programmes have helped to control vehicle emissions and enforce emission standards. However, progress in some low-income countries has been slow. Developing countries will not achieve benefits of advanced emission control technologies unless they implement cleaner fuel options.

In some Asian countries motorized two- and three-wheeled vehicles contribute disproportionately to emissions. However, regulations in some nations are reducing emissions from these vehicles. The shift from two-cycle to four-cycle engines, and the introduction of emission standards that effectively ban the sale of new vehicles powered by two-cycle engines will, in time, lead to a significant improvement in vehicle emissions.

Mass transport is an important alternative to private vehicles, and has been successfully implemented in many cities by using light rail, underground and rapid bus transit systems. Fuel switching from diesel to compressed natural gas has been implemented for public transport vehicles in cities such as Delhi and Cairo, leading to reductions in emissions of particulate matter and SO_2. In many countries, widespread use of mass transport continues to be hampered, however, by inefficiency and negative perceptions.

Industrial and Energy Sector Emissions

In many developed countries emissions from large industrial sources have been controlled by fuel changes and emission control laws. The reduction of SO_2 emissions in Europe and North America has been one of the success stories of recent decades. Agreements such as the 1979 UNECE [United Nations Economic Commission for Europe] Convention on Long-Range Transboundary Air Pollution played an important role in this success. The ECE convention adopted the concept of critical loads (thresholds in the environment) in 1988 and, in 1999, the Gothenburg Protocol [to Abate Acidification, Eutrophication, and Ground-level Ozone] set targets for national emissions of SO_2, NO_x, NH_x [a protein] and VOCs [volatile organic compounds]. In Europe, SO_2 has been reduced considerably, partly due to these agreements. It is also the result of policies calling for cleaner fuels, flue gas desulphurization and new industrial processes. Emissions also fell as the result because of the demise of many heavy industries, particularly in Eastern Europe and the former Soviet Union. However, SO_2 emissions have increased in many developing country regions.

Stricter environmental regulation and economic instruments, such as emissions trading, have triggered the introduction of cleaner technologies, and promoted further technological innovation.

Economic policies send important signals to producers and consumers. For example, Europe is shifting from taxing labour to taxing energy use to better reflect the impacts of emissions. Other successful examples include cap-and-trade policies in the United States to reduce SO_2 emissions from power plants. International use of such economic instruments is growing. Many cleaner technologies and cleaner production options are mature and commercially available, but there is great need for global cooperation regarding technology transfer to make them more widely available.

Indoor Air Quality

With some 1.6 million people dying prematurely each year from exposure to polluted indoor air, many developing countries in Africa, Asia and Latin America have attempted to address the emissions from the burning of biomass fuels and coal indoors. Responses include providing households with improved stoves; cleaner fuels, such as electricity, gas and kerosene; and information and education to make people aware of the impacts of smoke on the health of those exposed, especially women and young children. A modest shift from solid biomass fuels, such as wood, dung and agricultural residues, to cleaner fuels has been achieved, and governments have supported such measures, but further progress along such lines is urgently necessary if any major advances are to be realized.

European Air Quality Is Improving by Reducing Emissions

European Environment Agency (EEA)

The European Environment Agency (EEA) is a European Union entity responsible for providing accurate and independent environmental information. In the following viewpoint, the agency describes the actions the European Union (EU) has implemented to reduce emissions, including setting legally binding limits on each member state. The agency argues that this is needed to further improve air quality in Europe.

As you read, consider the following questions:

1. How many EU member states will miss one or more of their 2010 targets to reduce harmful air pollutants?
2. According to the latest EEA data, what percentage of Europe's urban population may have been exposed to concentrations of particulate matter above the EU limit?
3. For what four pollutants does the National Emissions Ceiling Directive (NECD) set limits?

*T*he characters in this story are fictional. However the data are real. The story is set on 27 July 2008 when an air quality warning was issued in Brussels.

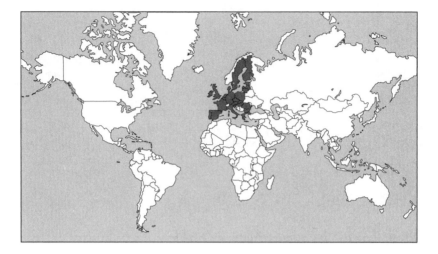

Anna is 37 years old and lives in the centre of Brussels. She and her young son Johan are planning a trip outside the busy city. Anna suffers from asthma and her doctor has warned of the dangers of air pollution, especially on hot summer days. Anna has heard about the London fogs of the 1950s that killed 2,000 people in one week. She has childhood memories of evening news bulletins showing dead fish and dying trees as 'acid rain' first came to popular attention in the 1970s. Motherhood and a recent asthma attack have quite rightly brought air pollution back to mind. The fact is that emissions of many air pollutants have fallen substantially across Europe since Anna's childhood. The air she and Johan breathe is much improved compared to the past, and air policy is one of the great success stories of the EU's [European Union's] environmental efforts. In particular, EU policy has dramatically cut emissions of sulphur, the main component of 'acid rain'.

In contrast, nitrogen—also a major component of 'acid rain'—has not been dealt with to the same extent and so continues to cause major problems. A significant proportion of Europe's urban population still lives in cities where EU air quality limits, protecting human health, are regularly exceeded.

Each year, many more people die prematurely from air pollution in Europe than die in traffic accidents. The European goal of achieving levels of air quality that do not damage people's health or the environment has still not been reached. EEA [European Environment Agency] analysis suggests that 15 of the 27 EU member states will miss one or more of their legally binding 2010 targets to reduce harmful air pollutants.

The European goal of achieving levels of air quality that do not damage people's health or the environment has still not been reached.

Particulate Matter and Ozone

Two pollutants, fine particulate matter and ground-level ozone, are now generally recognised as the most significant in terms of health impacts. Long-term and peak exposure can lead to a variety of health effects, ranging from minor irritation of the respiratory system to premature death.

Particulate matter, a term used to describe a variety of tiny particles from sources such as vehicle exhausts and domestic stoves, affect the lungs. Exposure can harm people of all ages, but people with existing heart and respiratory problems are particularly at risk.

According to the latest EEA data, since 1997 up to 50% of Europe's urban population may have been exposed to concentrations of particulate matter above the EU limit set to protect human health. As much as 61% of the urban population may have been exposed to levels of ozone that exceed the EU target. It has been estimated that $PM_{2.5}$ (fine particulate matter) in air has reduced statistical life expectancy in the EU by more than eight months.

The EEA has noted that while emissions of these two key air pollutants have dropped since 1997, measured concentrations in the air we breathe have remained largely the same. As yet, we don't know why there has not been a drop in ambient

Climate Change Mitigation Efforts Will Improve Air Quality

In January 2008, the European Commission proposed a Climate and Energy package to:

- reduce greenhouse gas emissions by 20% by 2020;

- increase the share of renewable energy by 20% by 2020;

- improve energy efficiency by 20% by 2020.

The efforts required to meet these targets will also cut air pollution in Europe. For example, improvements in energy efficiency and increased use of renewable energy will both lead to reduced amounts of fossil fuel combustion—a key source of air pollution. These positive side effects are referred to as the 'co-benefits' of climate change policy. It has been estimated that the above package will cut the cost of meeting EU [European Union] air pollution targets by EUR 8.5 billion per year. The savings to the European health services could be as much as six times that figure.

European Environment Agency,
"Every Breath You Take—Air Quality in Europe,"
March 2, 2009. www.eea.europa.

concentrations but it could be a combination of several factors: increased temperatures caused by climate change could be affecting air quality; perhaps we are on the receiving end of pollution from other continents or natural emissions of ozone-forming substances released from trees, for example.

A Day in the Country

Anna is planning a day in the country with Johan. Before leaving her apartment, she logs onto IRCEL, a government

Web service providing a host of regular information on air quality around Belgium. Using maps, Anna can scan readings and forecasts for particulate matter, ozone, nitrogen dioxide, sulphur dioxide among many others. The data are relayed to the Web from monitoring stations around the country.

Improvements in monitoring and availability of information on air pollution are another of the success stories of recent years. For instance, local data on ozone levels are now passed onto the EEA 'Ozone Web' service that provides an overview of the situation across Europe.

Anna scrolls across a map of Belgium, zooming in on a monitoring station in the centre of Brussels, less than two kilometres from her home.

The reading, taken minutes earlier, shows high levels of ozone in Brussels. Indeed the website forecasts that levels will exceed EU target values later that day and again the following day.

Anna leaves her apartment building and makes for the nearest Metro station, a 10-minute walk away. Out on the street, the full impact of the city's traffic problems are easy to see—and smell.

Exhaust emissions from cars in the centre of Brussels, and all major cities, irritate the respiratory tract and eyes and lungs. Anna and Johan turn into their local train station and head for the countryside.

Soon, Anna and Johan are entering a national park just outside Brussels. A sign tells them that they are visiting a Natura 2000 site—one part of a European-wide ecological network, set up to secure natural habitats and to maintain the range of plant and animal life.

Nitrogen

But what's that smell? A tractor is spraying liquid manure onto a field not far away. This is irritating, Anna thinks, but it's also part of real country life which is shown in a rather more romantic way in Johan's picture books.

The pungent smell is caused by as many as 40 different chemical substances emitted from the manure. Ammonia (NH_3), a volatile nitrogen compound, is one of them. In very high concentrations NH_3 is caustic and can damage the respiratory tract. However, the levels here are not dangerous for human health. Anna can breathe a sigh of relief, albeit a stinky one.

Nitrogen is an essential nutrient in nature. Reactive nitrogen forms are actually used by our bodies to produce proteins. However, excess nitrogen can lead to severe environmental and health problems.

'Acid rain' forms when high levels of sulphur and nitrogen oxides are present in the air. One of the great success stories of air pollution policy over the last decades has been the massive reduction in emissions of sulphur dioxide. The 32 EEA member countries reduced sulphur emissions by 70% between 1990 and 2006. Nitrogen, on the other hand, has not been dealt with as successfully.

With sulphur emissions declining, nitrogen is now the principal acidifying component in our air. Agriculture and transport are the main sources of nitrogen pollution. Agriculture is responsible for more than 90% of ammonia (NH_3) emissions alone.

Suddenly Johan, who has been walking unsteadily loses his balance and falls into a clump of stinging nettles. Having picked him up and brushed him off, Anna notices nettles everywhere. She has vivid memories of them as a child in a neighbour's garden. Then the nettles grew around a compost heap that was also used as a dump for poultry dung. That was no coincidence—the stinging plant is an indicator of high nitrogen concentrations in soils.

'Eutrophication' is the most likely cause of this explosion of stinging nettles surrounding Johan. It occurs when too many chemical nutrients . . . are available to an ecosystem either on land or in water. In water, excessive plant growth and subsequent decay occur, which in turn leads to further effects including oxygen depletion. Fish and other animals and plants ultimately suffocate as the oxygen supply is used up.

The abundance of the nettles here suggests that despite being a protected habitat, the Natura 2000 site is not immune from airborne nitrogen deposits. The fence protecting the area offers no defence—in fact building a greenhouse around the area would be the only way to protect it totally from airborne substances.

Looking Ahead

Because air pollution pays no regard to national boundaries the problem needs to be tackled internationally. The United Nations Convention on Long-Range Transboundary Air Pollution (LRTAP Convention) agreed in 1979, has been signed by 51 countries and forms the basis of the international fight to tackle air pollution.

In parallel, the EU has developed polices limiting the total emissions of each member state, setting legally binding limits. The 'National Emissions Ceiling Directive' (NECD) is a key EU policy. It sets 'ceilings' or limits for four pollutants: sulphur dioxide (SO_2), nitrogen oxides (NO_x), non-methane volatile organic compounds (NMVOCs), and ammonia (NH_3). Member states should meet these ceilings by 2010.

Because air pollution pays no regard to national boundaries the problem needs to be tackled internationally.

The EEA considers that further emission cuts are still needed in order to properly protect environment and health. An EEA analysis of the most recent NECD data indicates that 15 member states expect to miss at least one of their four ceilings; with 13 anticipating missing ceilings for the 2 nitrogen-containing pollutants NO_x and NH_3.

In 2009 the European Commission plans to publish a proposal to revise the current NECD, including stricter ceilings for the year 2020. National limits are likely to be proposed for fine particulate matter ($PM_{2.5}$) for the first time.

The NECD is mirrored by air quality directives, setting limit and target values for major air pollutants. A new one called the Cleaner Air for Europe (CAFE) directive was adopted in April 2008. For the first time it sets legally binding limit values for $PM_{2.5}$ concentrations (fine particulate matter), to be attained in 2015. The European Commission is also taking countries to task for having missed earlier limits and, where sufficient measures have not been outlined to improve performance, has begun infringement proceedings.

Later that evening Anna, while watching the evening news, sees that an air quality warning has been issued by the government in response to high ozone levels beyond the EU threshold. The warning advises people with breathing problems to take precautions such as avoiding strenuous exercise while the ozone levels remain high.

China Struggles to Improve Air Quality

Andreas Lorenz

Andreas Lorenz is a contributor to Der Spiegel, *a German news-weekly. In the following viewpoint, he describes several of the environmental measures that China has implemented to cut the alarmingly high levels of air pollution at Olympic sites in Beijing before the start of the 2008 Olympic Games. Lorenz reports that environmentalists are concerned that Chinese officials are covering up how bad Beijing's air pollution is.*

As you read, consider the following questions:

1. What is the population of China?
2. How much has the Chinese government spent over the past several years to keep its "green games" pledge?
3. How many monitoring stations were set up to supply air quality data in Beijing?

Down in the courtyard there's a silver-colored building made of corrugated sheet metal that looks something like a missile control center. Inside, large screens hang on the wall with position lights and graphs showing current cloud formations throughout China. Double rows of scientists in white coats sit silently in front of computers and compile data.

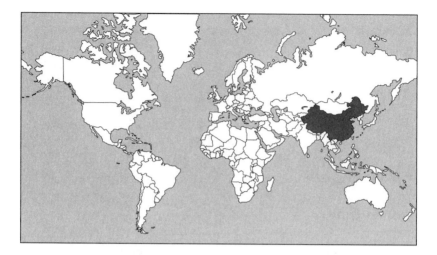

Wang Chunlin, a man with a stubble haircut, is in a good mood. The engineer employed by the Beijing Municipal Bureau of Environmental Protection has great news: "We're going to have clean air. August and September are always the best time of the year anyway."

Wang smiles, aware of the importance of his forecasts. His country is in urgent need of favorable environmental prognoses.

A recent measurement taken near the Olympic stadium showed that the concentration of dust particles in the air there was five times higher than the limit recommended by the World Health Organization (WHO).

Global Concern over Air Quality

The Olympic Games are scheduled to get under way in Beijing in just three weeks time [August 8–24 2008]. And the question of the weather and environmental conditions in the Chinese capital is probably one of the biggest issues preoccupying people around the world right now.

Beijing, with a population of 17 million, is one of the world's most polluted cities. On days when there is smog people on the street take to wearing filter masks. A recent measurement taken near the Olympic stadium showed that the concentration of dust particles in the air there was five times higher than the limit recommended by the World Health Organization (WHO). Many of the athletes who will be competing for medals in Beijing are uneasy about this. Those who will be taking part in endurance disciplines are particularly worried about health issues and reduced ability to realize their potential. Experts already feel certain that many track-and-field athletes will not be able to put in their best performances due to air pollution.

When smog forms the Forbidden City disappears behind a wall of gray.

The hosts, on the other hand, continue to give their assurances that things aren't half as bad as they're being made out to be. The Chinese government promised the International Olympic Committee (IOC) it would organize "green games." Massive measures of a kind only possible in a totalitarian system (including plant closures and driving bans) are being taken to avoid the embarrassment of seeing cyclists or runners coughing and wheezing as they struggle to make it to the finish line.

Last Thursday was the kind of day the Chinese government is hoping to have for the Olympics. A sunny blue sky over Beijing with hardly a cloud to be seen and the western mountains clearly visible in the distance. Tourists could be seen taking pictures of each other in front of the "Bird's Nest," the new national stadium. Absolutely superb weather in China's capital.

Beijing in August

However, the truth of the matter is that Beijing is normally more like a giant sauna in August. The temperature goes up to around 40 degrees Celsius (104 degrees Fahrenheit), the humidity is high, and a gray haze hangs in the air. Between August 8th and 24th last year [2007] there was not a single day when the air quality was in compliance with WHO guidelines.

When smog forms the Forbidden City disappears behind a wall of gray. Only vague outlines can be seen from the new futuristic television center on the 3rd Ring Road despite its proximity. The western mountains are just a distant memory.

The city's residents cough, their eyes burn, a sticky wet film forms on everything. Dust particles, nitrous oxide, and sulfur dioxide concentrations rise to dramatic levels. The authorities send out text messages to warn asthma sufferers to stay indoors and close the windows.

"My five-year-old son has had a chronic sore throat since he was two years old. He has to clear his throat all the time," says Beijing secretary Wang Hongmei. "That's because of the air pollution."

Part of this foul mixture comes out of the exhaust pipes of the more than three million cars that jam the streets of Beijing day in and day out. Although the city government has imposed European standards for exhaust emissions, so many new vehicles are registered every day that even the strictest rules can't help.

Bringing Beijing to a Halt

Another problem is the fact that numerous factories and power stations are located in residential areas. They're a curse from the past, a legacy Beijing owes to Mao Zedong, the founder of the modern Chinese state. Mao saw smokestacks and factory buildings side by side with residential housing and cultural centers as a socialist ideal.

Smokestacks belonging to power stations even protrude into the sky close to the Olympic park. On the outskirts of the city there are dozens of steel mills and chemicals plants busily contributing to China's economic growth. Under adverse wind conditions streets, office buildings and apartment blocks are shrouded in the foul-smelling gases they give off. When sand blows in from the Gobi Desert and mixes with the fine dust that is stirred up all year round at the countless construction sites in and around Beijing the air turns a brownish-yellow color and triggers fits of coughing in people exposed to it.

The government spent the equivalent of €10.7 billion ($16.8 billion) over the past several years in an effort to keep its "green games" pledge. Factories were relocated, subway lines built, outdated boilers replaced. In addition, special plans have been made for when the games actually begin. The idea is to bring half of the city to a grinding halt.

On Sunday numerous construction sites and gas stations were shut down. Factories have had to close or reduce their emissions by a third. For the next two months a special driving ban will be in place in Beijing with cars only allowed to be driven every other day. Around 300,000 vehicles that do not meet current exhaust emission standards cannot be driven at all. No burning of grass or straw will be allowed on the fields around Beijing.

Positive Changes

Environmentalists have praised these measures. White smoke billows out of the chimney of a coal-fired power plant in Beijing's Chaoyang District. "We've installed new scrubbers," Deputy Director Yu reports proudly. "We've been able to reduce our sulfur dioxide emissions to 20 milligrams per cubic meter. Just as the government requires."

But will measures like this be enough? "Go to the botanical gardens more often," was the advice I got not long ago from a senior Environment Ministry official who asked to remain anonymous. "Everywhere else the dust particle concentrations are so high that I'm not allowed to disclose them."

The blue dots on the graphic display at the Beijing Air Pollution Index (API) makes it look like an aquarium in which bubbles are rising to the surface. On many days between March 2007 and June 2008 concentrations ranged between 100 and 200 API points. On others they reached the 500 mark, constituting a significant danger to public health.

Wang Chunlin, the man from Beijing's Environmental Protection Bureau, is very self-confident. His office has its own set of definitions for clean and dirty air. For Wang the sky is blue when the API is at 100. When scientists in Hong Kong speak of "slight pollution" Beijing reports "excellent" air quality for the same measurements.

A "Disinformation Campaign"

A propaganda battle is being fought over pollution measurements. Reporters stand in front of the Olympic stadium with measuring instruments and tell the world that every breath drawn here will make you sick. Wang and his people are doing everything they can to counteract this impression.

A total of 27 monitoring stations were set up to supply air quality data for the Olympic Games host city. And recently the message has mostly been that everything is just fine. However, an American scientist, Steven Andrews, noticed that two monitoring stations were removed from locations where there is a high volume of traffic and three new ones were set up at locations where pollution levels are lower.

Andrews also found out that the pollution standards were secretly lowered, that changes were made with regard to substances being measured, and that some substances, such as ozone, were simply not measured at all. Andrews spoke of a disinformation campaign. He says there is every reason to believe that Beijing's effort to ensure that the Olympic Games will be "green" is headed for failure. In his view, all that China has succeeded in doing thus far is to find clever ways of covering up its inability to reduce pollution levels.

According to David Martin, exercise physiologist and respiratory expert for the US marathon team, breathing the air in Beijing could be compared to "feeding an athlete poison."

A Danger to Athletes?

The athletes, whose performances will hopefully make the Beijing Olympics a sports fest of superlatives, are perturbed by the situation. Many of them, including the German, British, and Swedish track-and-field teams, have chosen not to come to Beijing to prepare for the games and have gone to Japan or South Korea instead. "We want to wait as long as possible before exposing ourselves to the pollution there," says German high jumper Eike Onnen. The Olympic teams from the Netherlands and Switzerland have gone to the coastal city of Dalian for pre-competition training. Most teams plan to fly to Beijing shortly before the games begin.

According to David Martin, exercise physiologist and respiratory expert for the US marathon team, breathing the air in Beijing could be compared to "feeding an athlete poison." Ethiopian world record holder Haile Gebrselassie decided to withdraw from the marathon and will only be competing in the 10,000 meters. He suffers from asthma and was afraid that running the longer distance in the conditions that currently exist in Beijing could be harmful to his health. American boxing team physician Frank Filiberto accompanied 11 boxers to Beijing for a competition last November. On their first morning in the city his charges returned from a 20-minute run complaining of burning eyes and breathing problems: "In my opinion boxers are probably the finest athletes in the world," Filiberto said. "But they didn't think they could make it three rounds in Beijing."

The IOC has tried to play down the importance of the problem. After all, even Greenpeace finds China's environmental legislation "progressive." IOC officials say that the marathon and triathlon could be postponed if air pollution levels are particularly high on the days the events are scheduled for.

Mysterious Algae

But then pictures suddenly emerged that couldn't be denied. A gigantic carpet of algae appeared in front of the city of Qingdao, right in the bay where the Olympic sailing events are scheduled to take place.

Where the algae came from remains unknown. A random natural phenomenon? Or the result of the poor water quality in the region caused by pollutant discharges and excessive use of fertilizers over a period of decades?

Thousands of soldiers and volunteers spent several days fishing tons of green algae out of the water and then built protective fences around the regatta course. Disaster seems to have been averted for the time being, but no one is certain a renewed algae bloom can be prevented.

The problems facing Beijing's water supply have so far failed to attract much attention. Yet the city is drying out. More than two hundred rivers, streams, and canals are marked in blue on official maps. But when you go look for them what you often find is nothing but a dried-up bed where water used to be. This loss of natural waterways has affected the Shunyi District where the Olympic rowing and canoeing events are due to take place. The Chaobai River has been gone for many years now, with nothing but weeds and bushes growing in the dry riverbed.

Nevertheless the regatta course is now filled with three and a half meters of water. "It's fresh and clean. We're pumping it up out of the ground," says an employee of a company the local waterworks has commissioned to do the job.

Games Come at a Cost

The same method will ensure that a number of rivers and canals will be filled with water during the games. Environmentalists estimate that more than 200 million cubic meters of water will have to be pumped up out of the ground to be able to stage these sports events. Chinese farmers who are having to pump water up out of deep wells to irrigate their fields are the ones who will have to pay the price for this extravagance. "The games will inevitably exacerbate the water crisis," says environmentalist and regime critic Dai Qing.

However, it would seem that the need to keep up appearances is more important to the government. A new set of weather statistics appeared several days ago, stating that there is a high probability that the weather is going to be drizzly on August 8, the day of the opening ceremony.

Drizzly weather? That's unacceptable. The national weather service has made contingency plans to send up rockets filled with chemicals designed to dissipate rain clouds in the worst-case scenario. However, the ability of science to control the weather is limited. Meteorologist Chen Zhenlin concedes: "When it starts to come down real hard there's just not a whole lot we can do about it."

United Arab Emirates
Evaluates Air Quality

Khaleej Times

The Khaleej Times *is a daily English-language newspaper published in Dubai. In the following viewpoint, the staff discusses the findings of the United Arab Emirates' (UAE's) first State of the Environment Report, which finds that the country's oil and gas industry is the main source of air pollution in the region. The report concludes that air pollution in the UAE will continue to be a problem until the government finds an effective way to curb it.*

As you read, consider the following questions:

1. According to the report, where have nitrogen dioxide levels shot up in the United Arab Emirates?
2. When did the UAE stop importing CRCs and halon?
3. How many people live in Abu Dhabi?

The oil and gas industry is the main source of air pollution, followed by power and transportation sectors, according to the first State of the Environment Report, released by the Environment Agency-Abu Dhabi this month [March 2007].

Sulphur dioxide and particulate matter are causing concerns, the report says, adding that sulphur dioxide pollution is

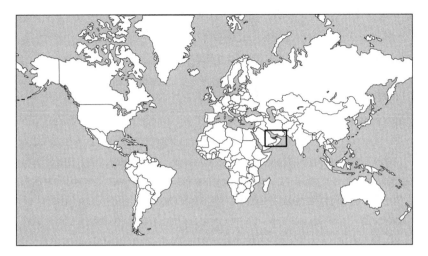

mainly a problem in Madinat Zayed, Habshan and Ruwais. Pollution levels in these areas are either close to or exceed air pollution limits.

Nitrogen dioxide levels have shot up in parts of Abu Dhabi city, Al Ain and Ruwais, according to the report. There is a relatively high, naturally occurring level of particulate matter in the air exceeding the air quality limits in areas like Mafraq, Shahama, Samha, Sas Al Nakhal and Al Ain, it adds.

The UAE has one of the highest per capita emission rates in the world, as per the [first State of the Environment] Report.

Emissions

The global mean temperature is rising because of emissions of greenhouse gases, mainly from fossil fuel consumption, it says.

The UAE [United Arab Emirates] has one of the highest per capita emission rates in the world, as per the report. Climate change may affect Abu Dhabi by raising the sea level, more flooding and extreme weather. Destruction of coral reef habitats has also been linked to climate change. Two episodes of coral bleaching took place in 1996 and 1998 in which live coral cover in some reefs declined by more than three-quarters. Recovery is now beginning to take place.

Ozone Layer

The ozone layer has been reduced on an average by three per cent since 1980 and an ozone hole is created over Antarctica during spring every year. Due to the Montreal Protocol [on Substances That Deplete the Ozone Layer] consumption of ozone depleting substances is decreasing globally and the ozone layer is expected to recover significantly by 2050. The UAE is in the process of phasing out the consumption of ozone depleting substances. Import of chlorofluorocarbons (CFCs) and halon will be banned in January 2010.

Furthermore, the report talks about how human beings have undoubtedly been having an impact on natural environments and biodiversity in the Arabian Gulf region for millennia. The earliest known archaeological sites within the Abu Dhabi date from over 7,000 years ago.

However, the severity of human impacts has increased enormously within recent years, and particularly during the past half century. This is thanks to the burgeoning human population and the extremely rapid rate of development since the coming of an oil-based economy in the 1960s, the report says.

The great majority of Abu Dhabi's 1.6 million or so inhabitants live in the coastal zone and it is here that human impacts are most directly felt, it says. However, people are increasingly also affecting the fragile, arid-land environments of the interior.

Fossils

The report also mentions that Abu Dhabi is very rich in archaeological and paleontological resources. Important fossils date to the Cretaceous period, between 66 and 144 million

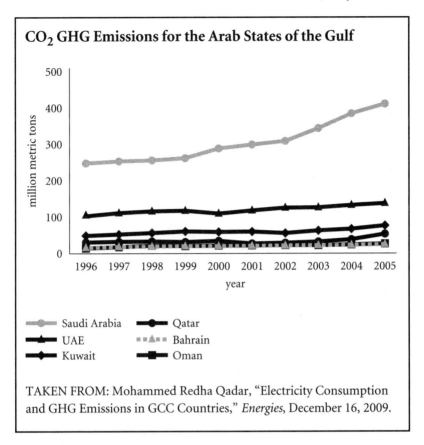

CO$_2$ GHG Emissions for the Arab States of the Gulf

TAKEN FROM: Mohammed Redha Qadar, "Electricity Consumption and GHG Emissions in GCC Countries," *Energies*, December 16, 2009.

years ago. The Baynunah formation, in the emirate's western region, has some of the world's best exposures of Late Miocene fossils from 6–8 million years ago.

Various examples of Bronze Age remains can be found. In fact, two Bronze Age chronological subdivisions—the Hafit period (3200–2600 BC) and the Umm al-Nar period (2600–2000 BC)—take their names from regions in the emirate.

Research also indicates that the 'falaj', an underground water channel system, was indigenous to the region around 3,000 years ago, during the Iron Age.

Currently, about six per cent of the emirate's total area is green by means of irrigation. This includes agricultural areas, forests, parks, gardens and roadside plantations.

Marine Resources

About the marine resources, the report says physical alterations such as land reclamation, dredging and the construction of breakwaters, along with increasing urban sprawl has resulted in the loss, degradation and fragmentation of coastal and marine habitats in Abu Dhabi.

Furthermore, urbanisation, which is being driven by a dramatic increase in the population growth rate, has led to increased pollution loads, particularly in the near shore area where the deterioration in water quality has impaired natural processes and the productivity of coastal ecosystems.

In addition to these, the waste treatment contributes to a number of environmental problems such as emissions of greenhouse gases, heavy metals and other environmentally hazardous chemicals. If not properly handled, landfills will leak and contaminate groundwater; gases [will] evaporate and contribute to global climate change; and toxic fumes will escape and threaten the health of people, says the report.

Singapore Assesses Air Quality

Singapore Ministry of the Environment and Water Resources

The Singapore Ministry of the Environment and Water Resources manages Singapore's natural resources and environmental policy. In the following viewpoint, the agency asserts that although Singapore has been rated highly for its air quality, there are increasing challenges in maintaining that level of success. This is the responsibility of not just government but also of developers and private industry.

As you read, consider the following questions:

1. According to a World Health Organization assessment, how many premature deaths occur every year because of the effects of air pollution?
2. What is the agency that monitors air quality and controls pollution in Singapore?
3. What system does Singapore use to measure ambient air quality?

Clean air is a prerequisite for a high standard of human health and well-being. However, air pollution continues to pose a serious threat to the health of people worldwide, particularly in developing countries. According to a World

Adapted from "Chapter 1: Air," *State of the Environment Yearbook 2008 Report*, Singapore Ministry of the Environment and Water Resources (MEWR), 2009, pp. 17–20, 22–25. Copyright © 2009 by National Environment Agency (NEA). Reproduced by permission.

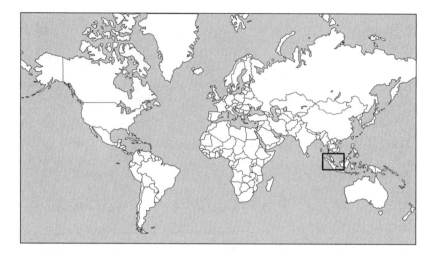

Health Organization (WHO) assessment, more than 2 million premature deaths each year can be attributed to the effects of air pollution.

In Singapore, our ambient air quality has been good and compares well with other urban cities in developed countries. In a 2005 survey by Political and Economic Risk Consultancy (PERC), Singapore was rated highly for our good air quality.

However, we face increasing challenges in maintaining our good ambient air quality. Singapore's population is increasing and our daily activities contribute to air pollution in one way or another. People are travelling more, resulting in increased traffic on the roads and higher vehicular emissions. More industries are being developed to sustain Singapore's growing economy and our competitiveness. All these will add to the domestic pollution load and have an impact on Singapore's ambient air quality. At the same time, we face occasional transboundary haze, which also affects our air quality during certain periods of the year.

Poor air quality inevitably takes a toll on the health of people. In contrast, cleaner air reduces one's risk of falling sick from pollutants in the air, especially for vulnerable groups with respiratory diseases. With cleaner air, we can have better public health and a better quality of life. Fresh air will also contribute to a cleaner environment that will help to attract potential investors, talents and tourists to Singapore.

Air may be free. But we cannot take for granted that the air we breathe will always remain fresh and clean. Clean air, besides land and water, is viewed as one of Singapore's precious resources. We must hence do our best to conserve clean air as a resource by reducing air pollution.

In Singapore, our ambient air quality has been good and compares well with other urban cities in developed countries.

Planning and Regulatory Controls

NEA [National Environment Agency] is the agency that monitors air quality and controls pollution in Singapore. NEA evaluates all proposed industrial developments to make sure that they do not pose any pollution problem. Through careful land-use planning, pollutive industries are sited away from residential and water catchment areas. Regulations are stringently enforced to ensure that industries implement proper measures to manage air pollution.

The agency regularly monitors the ambient air quality and looks out for potential air pollution incidents. NEA also regulates exhaust emissions from motor vehicles.

Pollutant Standards Index

Singapore's ambient air quality is measured using the Pollutant Standards Index (PSI) developed by the United States Environmental Protection Agency (USEPA).

In Singapore, the PSI is calculated from the concentrations of five key pollutants—particulate matter (PM_{10}), sulphur dioxide, ozone, carbon monoxide and nitrogen dioxide.

Health Impact of Air Pollution

PM_{10} refers to particulate matter such as dust or soot of 10 microns or smaller in size. 10 microns is about one-fifth the thickness of a strand of human hair. There are studies to show that breathing in PM_{10} can cause respiratory problems and be potentially dangerous, especially to the elderly and those suffering from asthma. In Singapore, the main sources of PM_{10} are exhaust fumes from motor vehicles (diesel vehicles in particular), power plants and factories. Studies have shown that a subset of PM_{10}, very fine particulate matter of 2.5 microns or smaller in size ($PM_{2.5}$), poses an even greater health threat due to its size.

Sulphur dioxide is a colourless gas that smells like burnt matches. It affects the lungs and may result in the burning of the nose and throat, breathing difficulties and severe airway obstructions at high concentration levels. Factories and power plants are the main sources of sulphur dioxide emissions in Singapore.

Excessive exposure to carbon monoxide can cause carbon monoxide poisoning, while nitrogen dioxide can irritate the lungs and render a person susceptible to respiratory problems like flu. For those who are already having respiratory problems like asthma, nitrogen dioxide may aggravate their condition. High ozone levels can cause severe asthma attacks and other respiratory health problems, especially for children and the elderly. Levels of carbon monoxide, nitrogen dioxide and ozone are relatively low in Singapore.

Taking Greater Responsibility

NEA reviews its regulations regularly to ensure that its standards remain relevant in the local context and are in line with international developments. However, the responsibility does not just lie with the Government—everyone has a role to play to keep the air free from pollution. Developers proposing to build factories must carry out their own pollution control as-

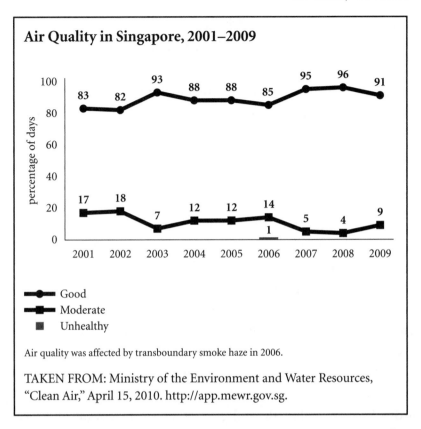

Air Quality in Singapore, 2001–2009

Air quality was affected by transboundary smoke haze in 2006.

TAKEN FROM: Ministry of the Environment and Water Resources, "Clean Air," April 15, 2010. http://app.mewr.gov.sg.

sessment studies. Factories in operation should also monitor and ensure compliance with emission standards set by the government. In the event of any violation, they must notify the authorities and at the same time, take measures to correct the problem. In addition, industries are encouraged to adopt green technologies, e.g., using cleaner fuels such as natural gas, and installing more efficient pollution control equipment. The industry can hence help to fulfill its social responsibility by reducing its emissions.

Key Challenges: Diesel Vehicles & PM$_{2.5}$

A key pollutant of concern for Singapore is PM$_{2.5}$, which currently does not meet the USEPA standards. Diesel vehicles contribute about 50% of PM$_{2.5}$ in Singapore. Through various policy measures that would help reduce emissions from diesel vehicles, we aim to meet USEPA standards of 15 µg/m3 by 2014.

Since 1 October 2006, all new diesel-powered vehicles have to comply with the Euro IV emission standards. In February 2007, we further extended the accelerated depreciation tax allowance scheme, which aimed to encourage existing vehicle owners to switch from older pre-Euro IV diesel vehicles to Euro IV-compliant diesel vehicles.

We also encourage the use of green vehicles, which are less pollutive than conventional petrol- and diesel-driven vehicles. Green Vehicle Rebates were first introduced in January 2001 for electric and hybrid vehicles, and extended to CNG [compressed natural gas] vehicles in October 2001. However, the initial take-up was modest, with 198 green vehicles on the roads as of end 2005. The scheme has since been enhanced (with the rebate off the additional registration fee doubled to 40% of the open market value for passenger cars and taxis from January 2006). By end 2007, there were a total of 1,549 green vehicles on Singapore's roads (1,062 hybrid cars, 486 CNG vehicles and 1 electric car). The Government has also announced that the Green Vehicle Rebate scheme will be further extended to 2009.

The Chassis Dynamometer Smoke Test (CDST) has been used to test diesel vehicles that have been booked for smoke emission by NEA's enforcement team since 1 September 2000. The proportion of smoky diesel vehicles plying our roads has reduced from 1.1% in 2000 to 0.3% in 2007. Results show that the CDST is an effective test for weeding out smoky diesel vehicles. To further reduce the number of smoky vehicles on the roads, all diesel-driven vehicles have to undergo the CDST during their mandatory periodic inspections from 1 January 2007.

Fazed by the Haze?

The annual land and forest fires in Indonesia have resulted in transboundary haze pollution that affects the ASEAN [Association of Southeast Asian Nations] subregion, with the 2006 haze episode being one of the worst since 1997. Apart from economic costs, the fog-like haze also affects the well-being of the people.

The fine dust particles in the haze irritate the nose, throat, airways, skin and eyes. Some also experience sneezing, runny nose, eye irritation, dry throat and dry cough from the air pollutants. Fortunately for most, the symptoms are mild and pose no grave danger to their health.

However, patients with medical problems like asthma, chronic lung disease, chronic sinusitis and allergic skin conditions may experience more severe symptoms. Children and the elderly in general, may also be more likely affected.

As the custodian of air quality in Singapore, NEA [National Environment Agency] will sustain its initiatives and strategies to safeguard air quality.

NEA closely monitors the haze situation. During severe haze conditions, the public is kept informed of the PSI [Pollutant Standards Index] at three-hourly intervals. Health authorities will also alert Singaporeans on preventive measures to take at such times.

On the international front, Singapore has been working closely with the Indonesian local authorities as well as relevant ASEAN countries to tackle the transboundary smoke haze. NEA assists the Indonesian authorities in their firefighting efforts by providing satellite pictures of hot spots to help them locate the fires on the ground. At the 10th ASEAN Ministerial Meeting on the Environment (AMME) held in the Philippines in November 2006, Singapore pledged US$50,000 to the ASEAN Haze Fund. In addition, Singapore accepted Indonesia's invitation to collaborate with the Muaro Jambi Regency to enhance its capacity to deal with land and forest fires.

As the custodian of air quality in Singapore, NEA will sustain its initiatives and strategies to safeguard air quality. What inspires and spurs us on is our desire to ensure that generations to come will continue to enjoy clear blue skies with clean and fresh air.

Iraq's Pressing Environmental Problems

Hayder Najm

Hayder Najm is a reporter for the Iraq weekly newsletter Niqash.
*In the following viewpoint, Najm contends that Iraq's political
parties are ignoring several increasingly serious air pollution
problems in favor of security and economic matters. Najm argues that many Iraqi citizens view environmental concern as a
luxury they cannot afford at this point.*

As you read, consider the following questions:

1. What did the United Nations Environment Programme
   report stress the need for in Iraq?
2. According to Ghassan al-Shamikhi, what have the wars
   of the past three decades brought to Iraq?
3. What do recent educational campaigns launched in Iraq
   aim to accomplish?

Iraq's political parties are neglecting environmental issues in
favor of other concerns, their policy projects and electoral
promises, launched ahead of legislative elections slated for
March 7 [2010], have made clear.

The agendas and identities of Iraq's political parties show,
according to political analyst Sumaya al-Musawi, that the en-

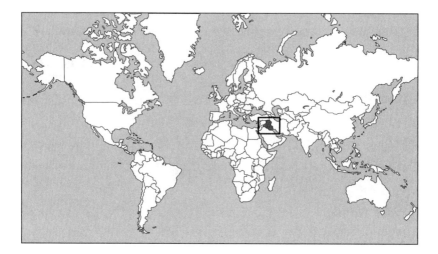

vironment is not a priority in Iraqi politics. There is no party currently focused on environmental protection, climate change or biodiversity.

Iraq is currently faced with a number of environmental crises, from polluted drinking water and drought to excessive radiological emissions, air pollution and desertification. Recent increases in these challenges have led some politicians to warn that they can no longer afford to be brushed aside in favor of focusing on security and political concerns alone.

Iraq is currently faced with a number of environmental crises, from polluted drinking water and drought to excessive radiological emissions, air pollution and desertification.

Policy Is Needed

"Environmental problems in Iraq require solutions and urgent responses," said Narmin Uthman, Environment Minister. "They require huge amounts of money and local government support as well as international assistance."

Uthman told *Niqash* that Iraq needed "collective and serious efforts by all government institutions, in order to face [up to] the grave environmental challenges."

Uthman argued that civil society organizations be granted a larger role in supervising and monitoring environmental protection and in spreading environmental awareness all over the country, but especially in the worst-hit areas.

A report recently issued by the United Nations Environment Programme stressed the need for a fast response to Iraq's environmental crisis, and highlighted the problems of war damage, an increase in medical waste and in rubbish piling, among other issues. The report said epidemics would follow if these were not addressed soon.

The report also said that water and sanitation systems urgently need improved maintenance to prevent further pollution of the environment.

Constant War Has Environmental Consequences

Ghassan al-Shamikhi, director of another monitoring organization, the Echo Center for Human Development, said that the wars of the past three decades have brought widespread pollution in their wake.

The attempt by Saddam Hussein's government to drain the marshland of southern Iraq, the use of depleted uranium by the invading US army (producing radioactive contamination) and the soil and agricultural pollution resulting from US military operations have heavily damaged the topsoil, exacerbating the existing problem of desertification.

Several civil and government institutions have launched educational campaigns to warn companies and citizens of the dangers of pollution and of the scale of the risk to Iraq and its people, risks such as epidemics among humans and livestock and damage to agriculture.

"These environmental problems deserve serious examination, particularly because losses resulting from air pollution and health problems are very costly to the national economy," said Ali Hannoush, former secretary-general of Iraq's Environment Ministry.

"The costs of treating patients and of medicine supply are very high," said Hannoush. "Not to mention the impact on the life cycles of patients."

Other Issues Take Priority

Jinan al-Ubaidi, an MP [member of Parliament] and member of the parliamentary health and environment committee, said that parties do not care much for the environment due to the many security, economic, and other challenges facing the country. Even ordinary citizens view environmental concern as a luxury, she added.

But this lack of interest "does not mean that all are not aware of the serious environmental crises, such as the drought that has recently hit the country," al-Ubaidi told *Niqash*.

"This will make them all allocate a space in their future projects to deal with such important and vital issues," she said.

Al-Ubaidi emphasized that the attention given by civil and government institutions to environmental protection continues to fall short given the scale of the environmental challenges facing Iraq.

She highlighted a recent law passed by the environment parliamentary committee which includes strict procedures for protecting the environment and reducing existing damage.

"We have developed a very strict law for environmental protection and granted the ministry of environment the needed powers to punish anyone who brings damage to the environment," said al-Ubaidi.

"We also formed the environmental police, tasked with punishing those who bring damage and pollution to the Iraqi environment," she added.

Critics say government action is yet to match its rhetoric as decision makers still do not attend scientific conferences on the relevant issues, sending only their representatives. Even they usually stay only for the opening speeches so as to make political capital out of their attendance.

Ukraine Cuts CO_2 Emissions, but Citizens See Little Difference

Kyiv Post

The Kyiv Post *is an English-language Ukrainian newspaper. In the following viewpoint, it asserts that although Ukraine has made key progress in cutting emissions in the past several years, that drop can be attributed to the economic downturn and the collapse of industry and is not the result of sound environmental policy.*

As you read, consider the following questions:

1. According to United Nations statistics, by how much has Ukraine decreased its CO_2 output from 1990 levels?
2. How many million carbon emission rights did Ukraine sell to Japan in 2009?
3. How many green projects have been approved by Ukraine's environmental agency?

D niprodzerzhynsk (Reuters)—Ukraine has made some of the world's deepest cuts in carbon emissions over the past two decades, but the ring of steel and chemical factories polluting her hometown make Natalya Maksymenko skeptical.

"This is not air—this is a horror," said the 25-year-old mother, screwing up her nose at the smoke belching out of

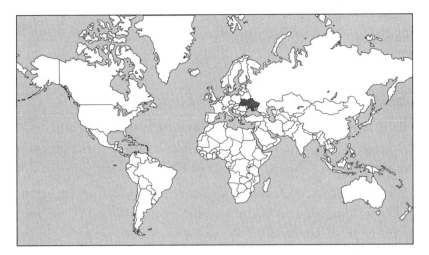

factory chimneys in Dniprodzerzhynsk, an industrial city of 250,000 people and birthplace of Soviet leader Leonid Brezhnev.

"We can even hear ourselves breathing in and out. You can see what is swimming in this air—carbon certainly and factory pollution. Everything is dirty," she complained.

Dirt-encrusted shop fronts stretch out a couple of kilometers along Lenin Avenue then end in a haze at a gigantic steel complex surrounded by swirling fumes.

It is hard to tell where the clouds end and the smoke begin in Dniprodzerzhynsk, a city which expanded rapidly under Soviet dictator Joseph Stalin's forced industrialization program.

Yet as leaders from around the world attempted to seal a deal on climate change in Copenhagen in early December, on paper Ukraine looks like a model pupil on CO_2 emissions reduction.

It has halved CO_2 output from 1990 levels to 345 million tons a year, according to U.N. statistics, allowing it to sell carbon emission rights it received under the Kyoto Protocol that are potentially worth billions of dollars.

But the reality is that Ukraine's plunging emissions have simply mirrored the collapse of its Soviet-era industry—the economy is still only three-quarters the size it was in 1990.

Control over Money

The global economic crisis accelerated that drop and the concern now is that this is killing the motivation to make greener power stations, factories and mines built 100 years ago.

Earlier this year, Ukraine sold 30 million carbon emission rights to Japan for $375 million and hopes to earn $2 billion or more from the sale of the right to pollute carbon credits that it does not use.

The reality is that Ukraine's plunging emissions have simply mirrored the collapse of its Soviet-era industry— the economy is still only three-quarters the size it was in 1990.

Viktor Khazan, a local environmentalist in Dniprodzer-zhynsk, says the 3 billion euros ($4.5 billion) Ukraine could make from its sale of CO_2 rights is being wasted rather than spent on green projects, as intended by the Kyoto rules.

"There were projects where the funds were partially used and the rest went to altogether other uses," he said. "As long as there is no control over organizations, political parties, we can't say the money will be used only (on ecological projects)."

Mykola Sasiuk, the deputy head of Ukraine's environmental investment agency that sells CO_2 rights, denies this. He says 150 projects have been outlined, with 30 approved.

"These projects are already working and have produced real reductions (in emissions)," he said.

Ukraine's largest coal mine, Zasyadko, for example, had cut emissions by 4 million tons, he said.

But for some in Dniprodzerzhynsk, the projects have come far too late.

"I was poisoned by coking coal fumes and after that I could not go to work at the factory because it affected my health badly," said unemployed former steelworker Viktor, 37.

"We don't have the power to change anything," he said with a shrug as he fished from a bridge over the Dnipro River that gives the town its name.

Periodical and Internet Sources Bibliography

The following articles have been selected to supplement the diverse views presented in this chapter.

Heather Cannon-Winkelman	"Our One and Only Planet, What Can We Expect from COP15," *Daily Observer* (Liberia), December 10, 2009.
Tony Carnie	"Sapref Manages to Reduce Emissions," *Daily News* (South Africa), August 13, 2010.
Thomas Chan	"Time to Change Anti-Pollution Policy," *China Daily*, August 13, 2010.
Ed Douglas	"Why Dmitry Medvedev Should Turn His Attention to Russia's Peat Bogs," *Guardian* (UK), August 7, 2010.
EUbusiness	"Stockholm's Green City Award: It's What You Can't See That Counts," April 4, 2010. www.eubusiness.com.
Sudipto Mondal	"Mangalore Is the Most Polluted Industrial City in Karnataka," *Hindu* (India), January 16, 2010.
Ana Maria Nitoi	"Power Balance Shifts to Green," *Diplomat* (Romania), February 2009.
Arjun Ramachandran	"Sydney Dust Blanket Causes Highest Air Pollution on Record," *Sydney Morning Herald*, September 23, 2009.
Sydney Morning Herald	"Air Quality in Sydney Breaches Safe Levels 19 Times," January 17, 2010.
John Vidal	"London Air Pollution 'Worst in Europe,'" *Guardian* (UK), June 25, 2010.
Jin Zhu	"Air Quality Drops in First Half of Year," *China Daily*, July 27, 2010.

GLOBALVIEWPOINTS

CHAPTER 2

The Health Effects of Air Pollution

Global Assessment of the Issue of Indoor Air Pollution

World Health Organization (WHO)

The World Health Organization (WHO) is the United Nations organization responsible for directing and coordinating health research and policy. In the following viewpoint, WHO explores the serious problem of indoor air pollution, which disproportionately affects women and children in developing countries. WHO also discusses the research and policies that it is developing to address the issue of indoor air pollution.

As you read, consider the following questions:

1. What percentage of the world's population relies on dung, wood, crop waste, or coal to meet basic energy needs?
2. How many deaths per year are caused by indoor air pollution?
3. What percentage of deaths attributed to indoor air pollution occur in children under five years of age?

Scope of the Problem

More than half of the world's population rely on dung, wood, crop waste or coal to meet their most basic energy needs. Cooking and heating with such solid fuels on open fires or stoves without chimneys leads to indoor air pollution. This indoor smoke contains a range of health-damaging pollutants including small soot or dust particles that are able to penetrate deep into the lungs. In poorly ventilated dwellings, indoor smoke can exceed acceptable levels for small particles in outdoor air 100-fold. Exposure is particularly high among women and children, who spend the most time near the domestic hearth. Every year, indoor air pollution is responsible for the deaths of 1.6 million people—that's one death every 20 seconds.

The use of polluting fuels thus poses a major burden on the health of poor families in developing countries. The dependence on such fuels is both a cause and a result of poverty as poor households often do not have the resources to obtain cleaner, more efficient fuels and appliances. Reliance on simple household fuels and appliances can compromise health and thus hold back economic development, creating a vicious cycle of poverty.

In poorly ventilated dwellings, indoor smoke can exceed acceptable levels for small particles in outdoor air 100-fold.

According to the 2004 assessment of the International Energy Agency, the number of people relying on biomass fuels such as wood, dung and agricultural residues, for cooking and heating will continue to rise. In sub-Saharan Africa, the reliance on biomass fuels appears to be growing as a result of population growth and the unavailability of, or increases in the price of, alternatives such as kerosene and liquid petroleum gas. Despite the magnitude of this growing problem, the health impacts of exposure to indoor air pollution have yet to become a central focus of research, development aid and policy making.

The Health Impact: A Major Killer

The World Health Organization (WHO) has assessed the contribution of a range of risk factors to the burden of disease and revealed indoor air pollution as the 8th most important risk factor and responsible for 2.7% of the global burden of disease. Globally, indoor air pollution from solid fuel use is responsible for 1.6 million deaths due to pneumonia, chronic respiratory disease and lung cancer, with the overall disease burden (in Disability-Adjusted Life Years or DALYs, a measure combining years of life lost due to disability and death) exceeding the burden from outdoor air pollution fivefold. In high-mortality developing countries, indoor smoke is responsible for an estimated 3.7% of the overall disease burden, making it the most lethal killer after malnutrition, unsafe sex and lack of safe water and sanitation.

Indoor air pollution has been associated with a wide range of health outcomes, and the evidence for these associations has been classified as strong, moderate or tentative in a recent systematic review. Included in the above assessment were only those health outcomes for which the evidence for indoor air pollution as a cause was classified as strong. There is consistent evidence that exposure to indoor air pollution increases the risk of pneumonia among children under five years, and chronic respiratory disease and lung cancer (in relation to coal use) among adults over 30 years old. The evidence for a link with lung cancer from exposure to biomass smoke, and for a link with asthma, cataracts and tuberculosis was considered moderate. On the basis of the limited available studies, there is tentative evidence for an association between indoor air pollution and adverse pregnancy outcomes, in particular low birth weight, or ischaemic heart disease and nasopharyngeal and laryngeal cancers.

While the precise mechanism of how exposure causes disease is still unclear, it is known that small particles and several of the other pollutants contained in indoor smoke cause inflammation of the airways and lungs and impair the immune response. Carbon monoxide also results in systemic effects by reducing the oxygen-carrying capacity of the blood.

Pneumonia and Other Acute Lower Respiratory Infections. Globally, pneumonia and other acute lower respiratory infections represent the single most important cause of death in children under five years. Exposure to indoor air pollution more than doubles the risk of pneumonia and is thus responsible for more than 900,000 of the 2 million annual deaths from pneumonia.

Chronic Obstructive Pulmonary Disease. Women exposed to indoor smoke are three times as likely to suffer from chronic obstructive pulmonary disease (COPD), such as chronic bronchitis, than women who cook and heat with electricity, gas and other cleaner fuels. Among men, exposure to this neglected risk factor nearly doubles the risk of chronic respiratory disease. Consequently, indoor air pollution is responsible for approximately 700,000 out of the 2.7 million global deaths due to COPD.

Lung Cancer. Coal use is widespread in China and cooking on open fires or simple stoves can cause lung cancer in women. Exposure to smoke from coal fires doubles the risk of lung cancer, in particular among women who tend to smoke less than men in most developing countries. Every year, more than one million people die from lung cancer globally, and indoor air pollution is responsible for approximately 1.5% of these deaths.

Disproportionate Impacts on Children and Women

Household energy practices vary widely around the world, as does the resultant death toll due to indoor air pollution. While more than two-thirds of indoor smoke deaths from acute

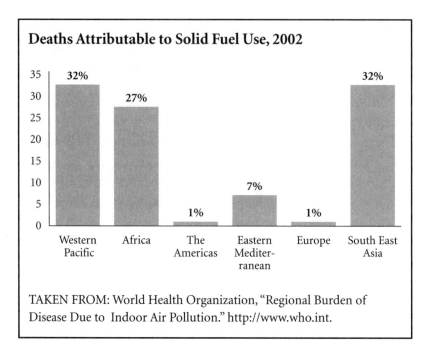

Deaths Attributable to Solid Fuel Use, 2002

TAKEN FROM: World Health Organization, "Regional Burden of Disease Due to Indoor Air Pollution." http://www.who.int.

lower respiratory infections in children occur in WHO's African and Southeast Asian regions, over 50% of the COPD deaths due to indoor air pollution occur in the Western Pacific region.

> *There is an urgent need to investigate which interventions work and how they can be implemented in a successful, sustainable and financially viable way.*

In most societies, women are in charge of cooking and—depending on the demands of the local cuisine—they spend between three and seven hours per day near the stove, preparing food. 59% of all indoor air pollution–attributable deaths thus fall on females. Young children are often carried on their mother's back or kept close to the warm hearth. Consequently, infants spend many hours breathing indoor smoke during their first year of life when their developing airways make them particularly vulnerable to hazardous pollutants. As a result, 56% of all indoor air pollution–attributable deaths occur in children under five years of age.

In addition to the health burden, fuel collection can impose a serious time burden on women and children. Alleviating this work will free women's time for productive endeavours and child care, and can boost children's school attendance and time for homework.

Millennium Development Goals Are Guiding International Action

Tackling indoor air pollution in the context of household energy is linked to achieving the Millennium Development Goals, in particular to reducing child mortality (Goal 4), to promoting gender equality and empowering women (Goal 3), to opening up opportunities for income generation and eradicating extreme poverty (Goal 1), and to ensuring environmental sustainability (Goal 7). WHO reports the "proportion of the population using solid fuels for cooking" as an indicator for assessing progress towards the integration of the principles of sustainable development into country policies and programmes. Yet, the central role of household energy is not currently reflected in the political responses to achieve the Millennium Development Goals.

Measures to reduce indoor air pollution and associated health effects range from switching to cleaner alternatives, such as gas, electricity or solar energy, to improved stoves or hoods that vent health-damaging pollutants to the outside, to behavioural changes. There is an urgent need to investigate which interventions work and how they can be implemented in a successful, sustainable and financially viable way.

What WHO Is Doing

WHO, as the global public health agency, is advocating for the integration of health in international and national energy policies and programmes. WHO collects and evaluates the evidence for the impact of household energy on health and for the effectiveness of interventions in reducing the health burden on children, women and other vulnerable groups. WHO's programme on household energy and health rests on four pillars:

- *Documenting the health burden of indoor air pollution and household energy:* WHO will provide a regular update of the links between household energy and health and, where feasible, offer support to key research undertakings.

- *Evaluating the effectiveness of technical solutions and their implementation:* Developing simple tools for monitoring the effectiveness of interventions in improving health and building the capacity to conduct such evaluations will help generate much-needed information from ongoing small- and large-scale projects. This information will provide the basis for the development of a catalogue of options that review both the effectiveness of interventions, and lessons learnt in relation to their implementation.

- *Acting as the global advocate for health as a central component of international and national energy policies:* Ultimately, policy makers will want to know whether it pays off to invest in large-scale operations to reduce indoor air pollution. In terms of health, a recent cost-effectiveness analysis of different interventions suggests that improved stoves and switching to kerosene and gas represent cost-effective solutions. In addition, WHO is working on a cost-benefit analysis of interventions that—beyond health—will take into account all the benefits associated with improved household energy practices.

- *Monitoring changes in household energy habits over time:* Information about the energy habits of poor, mostly rural households is scarce and WHO has the responsibility to work towards progress in this area and to report, on a yearly basis, the Millennium Development Goal indicator 29 "percentage of population using solid fuels".

Key partners include the Partnership for Clean Indoor Air, the United Nations Environment Programme, the United Nations Development Programme and the World Bank as well as many research institutions and nongovernmental agencies around the world. WHO is already actively taking part in projects in several developing countries, including the most sophisticated scientific indoor air pollution study to date undertaken in Guatemala, and work in China, Lao People's Democratic Republic, Mongolia, Nepal, Kenya and Sudan. In the future, work will focus even more on those countries and populations most in need.

United Kingdom Is Concerned About Deaths Caused by Air Pollution

Nina Lakhani

Nina Lakhani is a reporter for the Independent, *a daily British newspaper. In the following viewpoint, she states that the United Kingdom (UK) is failing to meet air quality standards set by the European Union (EU). Lakhani reports that although the UK has made progress in some areas, environmental groups believe that the British government must be much more proactive in implementing policies to further improve air quality.*

As you read, consider the following questions:

1. According to a parliamentary report, how many people are dying prematurely in the United Kingdom every year because of man-made air pollution?
2. How many people in England were exposed to unsafe levels of nitrogen oxides in 2007?
3. By what percentage have carbon dioxide emissions decreased since 1990?

More than 50,000 people are dying prematurely in the UK every year, and thousands more suffer serious illness because of man-made air pollution, according to a parliamen-

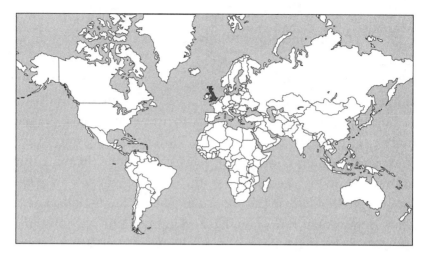

tary report published tomorrow. The UK now faces the threat of £300m in fines after it failed to meet legally binding EU targets to reduce pollution to safe levels.

Air pollution is cutting life expectancy by as many as nine years in the worst-affected city areas. On average, Britons die eight months too soon because of dirty air. Pollutants from cars, factories, houses and agriculture cause childhood health problems such as premature births, asthma and poor lung development. They play a major role in the development of chronic and life-shortening adult diseases affecting the heart and lungs, which can lead to repeated hospital admissions. Treating victims of Britain's poor air quality costs the country up to £20bn each year.

Nearly 5.5 million people receive NHS treatment for asthma, and more than 90,000 people were admitted to hospital as a result of the disease in England in 2008/09. US research has found that the lungs of children who live in highly polluted areas fail to develop fully.

Poor air quality is caused by three key pollutants—nitrogen oxides; particulate matter and ozone—where Britain fails to meet European safety targets.

Britain is Europe's worst emitter of nitrogen oxides and exposed 1.5 million people to unsafe levels in 2007, according to the World Health Organization (WHO). Long-term exposure can cause breathing problems, worsen asthma and bronchitis in children and aggravate allergies. They are by-products of burning fuel, and contribute to acid rain and make plants more susceptible to disease. Despite almost halving emissions since 1990, Britain is widely expected to fall short of the 2010 EU target for nitrogen oxides, which are a precursor to particulate matter (PM), the most dangerous of all pollutants. They play a major role in the development of chronic obstructive pulmonary disease in adults which will affect more people than heart disease by 2020.

Poor air quality is caused by three key pollutants—nitrogen oxides; particulate matter and ozone—where Britain fails to meet European safety targets.

Particulate matter is airborne and comes from materials ranging from sulphates, ammonia, carbon and water to mineral dust. Sources include coal burning, exhaust emissions, tyre wear, quarrying and construction. There is no safe level of PM; some people are affected by very low concentrations over a long period. It is also linked to heart disease and cancer.

Reduced coal use in the 1990s led to a 20 per cent reduction in PM, but a big increase in diesel vehicles on the road has seen progress stall since 2000. Eight areas, including Greater London, Swansea, and Yorkshire and Humberside have exceeded 2005 EU limits at least once. Last December, the EU rejected an application from the Department for Environment, Food and Rural Affairs (Defra) to give Greater London more time to meet the target after it was unable to prove the city had worked hard to meet the target.

Britain is also doing badly on ozone in the lower atmosphere, a toxin formed from chemical reactions between various air pollutants and sunlight. Ozone concentrations are rising in UK cities, though, generally, rural areas and sunnier climates fare worse. Ozone causes eye and skin irritations, reduces lung function and damages airways and can be deadly; ozone-related summer smog caused an additional 800 deaths in 2003. There is no legally binding EU limit but, in 2007, nearly 90 per cent of the UK population were exposed to levels above WHO recommendations.

The Commons Environmental Audit Committee (EAC) will tomorrow issue damning criticism of the UK's failure to prioritise air quality despite more than a decade of pressure from scientists and the EU. Ministers from all departments will be told that our air quality is "shameful", and they must "drive this from the top . . . and accept responsibility for policies that conflict with air quality".

The Government will also be asked to explain why millions of pounds have been spent raising awareness about obesity, passive smoking and alcohol, but not air quality—even though the costs to human life and the NHS are similar. The Government will also face pressure to instigate immediate cross-departmental action to address the country's air quality, in order to meet EU pollution targets, avoid spiralling fines and ultimately reduce the unnecessary deaths and illness that disproportionately affect people from lower socioeconomic groups.

Frank Kelly, professor of environmental health at King's College London, who gave evidence to the committee, said: "We have been banging this drum in the scientific community for 10 years and it now must be taken more seriously by the Government because this really is a damning report. . . . We must have an immediate major education campaign, because if people had an inkling about the impact of poor air quality on their children, then they would stop sitting outside the

---

UK Air Quality Can Be Improved

The quality of our air in the United Kingdom [UK] has improved considerably over the last decade. Overall, the air we breathe is cleaner today than at any time since before the Industrial Revolution. We have achieved this through tighter controls on emissions of pollutants from industry, transport and domestic sources. In recent years, our policies have helped cut concentrations of harmful pollutants and reduced the annual numbers of premature deaths and hospital admissions by many thousands. The long-term trend is of general improvement.

Despite this positive picture, air pollution still harms health and the environment. Recent research has shown that some pollutants are more dangerous than previously thought. For some pollutants there is no absolute safe threshold. Air pollution is currently estimated to reduce the life expectancy of every person in the UK by an average of 7–8 months with estimated equivalent health costs of up to £20 billion each year. Air pollution also has a detrimental effect on our ecosystems and vegetation. Clearly there are significant benefits to be gained from further improvements.

Jonathan Shaw,
"Ministerial Foreword," The Air Quality Strategy for England,
Scotland, Wales, and Northern Ireland: Volume 1,
July 2007. www.defra.gov.uk

---

school gates in their big cars and would be much more likely to help. Maybe the threat of enormous fines from the EU will finally get the Government's attention."

While the air quality in the UK has improved significantly over recent decades because of cleaner fuels, vehicles and improved industrial processes required by national and European laws, these improvements have levelled off or slowed down.

Londoners live with the worst air quality in Britain. Eight million people live amid millions of vehicles and close to several airports. But some policies targeted at improving air quality have been scrapped or delayed since the election of Boris Johnson as Mayor of London. These include plans to charge £25 per day for the biggest, heavy-polluting vehicles, and a westerly extension of the congestion charge.

Professor Kelly said: "Instead of tightening up our policies, they have been dismantled instead."

Londoners live with the worst air quality in Britain.

Environmental Protection UK, an influential campaign group, condemned what it called the Government's "wait and see" approach to air quality, which has meant pinning too much hope on the impact of European standards for cleaner vehicles.

Ed Dearnley, the group's policy officer, said yesterday: "Resources dedicated to air quality have been tiny in comparison to other areas of public health work such as obesity and passive smoking. Defra has struggled to get other departments, such as transport and health, to understand the problem and to act. The failure to get to grips with [more] vehicles on the roads, and the well-intentioned but counterproductive policies that have encouraged more diesel vehicles, means their 'wait and see' policy has failed."

A Defra spokeswoman said the EAC report described fines as "potential" not "expected". She added that the Government intends to avoid them by asking for more time to meet the limits. "Over the last few years there have been a range of measures introduced which demonstrate close working between departments. These include substantial investment in public transport and incentives through vehicle excise duty for less polluting vehicles," she said. "Of course, we accept that further measures are needed, and discussion is continuing on some of these."

In the Air: The UK's Cleanup Success Rate

Where we do well:

- Britain has never exceeded the EU lead target since it was set in 2007.

- The introduction of unleaded petrol in 1986 eradicated the main source of the highly toxic chemical.

- Carbon monoxide emissions have decreased by 75 per cent since 1990, largely as a result of catalytic converters in machinery and vehicles.

- Britain produced 16,800 tonnes of the cancer-causing benzene in 2007—a 72 per cent decrease since 1990. The EU target was met well in advance of the 2010 deadline.

Where we fail:

- Nitrogen oxide levels in some cities are 20 per cent higher than the European average. The 2010 target will not be met unless new national and local strategies are introduced.

- Although EU ambient air targets for ozone have been achieved, nearly 90 per cent of the country is exposed to levels considered too high by the World Health Organization.

- Polycyclic aromatic hydrocarbons increase risk of cancers. High levels were found in Scunthorpe in 2007, but the rest of the UK meets targets.

India Recognizes the Growing Problem of Indoor Air Pollution

Aruna Chandaraju

Aruna Chandaraju is a reporter for the Hindu, *India's national newspaper. In the following viewpoint, she elucidates the dangers of indoor air pollution (IAP), which is a major problem in India. Chandaraju reports that the worst affected are village women, who suffer severe health problems due to extended exposure to biomass smoke and other harmful pollutants.*

As you read, consider the following questions:

1. An estimated how many women and children die in India every year due to IAP-related causes?
2. What percentage of India's total energy supply is traditional biomass fuels?
3. What percentage of India's poultry farm workers have asthma?

You are in a busy public area: coughing or breathing in polluted air. Driving home in peak traffic, you curse as smoke and exhaust fumes assail you from all sides. But when you reach home, you shut the windows, switch on the fan, and relax, breathing a sigh of relief. Feeling safe finally.

But are you? Actually not. Right here too countless allergens and pollutants are possibly assailing you. You are being subject to Indoor Air Pollution (IAP).

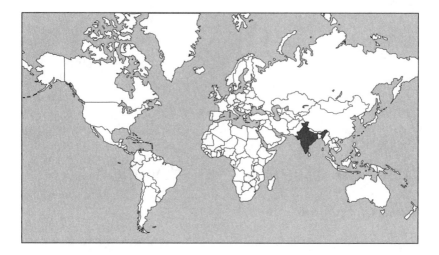

Health Problems

Few people know that because most studies, media attention
and public campaigns have focused on outdoor pollution. But
IAP is scarier than you could imagine. India currently has the
world's largest number of IAP-related health problems with 75
per cent of its households burning wood, dung cakes, and
crop residues (agricultural waste)—the "traditional" biomass
fuels. Also, an estimated 500,000 women and children die in
India each year due to IAP-related causes—25 per cent of estimated IAP-related deaths worldwide, according to a World
Bank report.

*There, probably, goes your romantic vision of villages
and rural homes as total havens of pure, fresh air.*

It is a massive problem considering that traditional biomass fuels account for over 50 per cent of India's total energy
supply, and 80 per cent of household energy supply. The worst
affected are villages and their women: They suffer severe health
problems due to extended exposure to biomass smoke and inhaling large quantities of harmful pollutants. Rural children,

especially girls, who typically stay with their mothers while the fathers and sons go out to work, are also at great risk of acute respiratory infection.

Studies by J.N. Pande, professor of medicine, All India Institute of Medical Sciences, New Delhi, show how unhealthy cooking methods and uses of biomass fuels not only contribute to respiratory tract infections, including chronic bronchitis in women, but also put children below five at grave risk. As he notes, even poor ventilation contributes: The smoke emitted during cooking has literally nowhere to go and so keeps circulating in the room itself.

There, probably, goes your romantic vision of villages and rural homes as total havens of pure, fresh air. However, if you believe you are safe because you live in a town or city, and spend your time at home and/or office with no burning-wood stoves around, think again. There are hazards in such atmospheres too.

Main Causes

Broadly, in urban India, the main IAP contributors are aerobiologicals and irritants. Aerobiologicals are dust mites, cockroaches, pollen and fungi, pet excreta, bacteria and viruses. It takes 100 dust mites per gm [gram] of dust to develop sensitivity and 500 dust mites per gm of dust to trigger coughing and wheezing according to Bangalore-based Dr. H. Paramesh, paediatric pulmonologist.

Even our kitchen trash bin contributes a huge volume of illness-causing bacteria and unpleasant odour to indoor air. Cockroach droppings trigger allergic asthma. In a study published in the *New England Journal of Medicine*, over half the homes tested had high numbers of cockroaches. Children in these homes were thrice as likely to be hospitalised for asthma. Even leakages in homes trigger allergies. Pets, especially their excreta and urine cause IAP. One reason why asthma is so high among Indian poultry farm workers (over 60 per cent) is because they are exposed to bird droppings, says Dr. Paramesh.

Irritants are carpets, heavy draperies, and cupboards made of compressed wood, which contain formaldehyde causing chronic eye irritation, cough and asthma. Granite emits radon that produces cough.

Even our kitchen trash bin contributes a huge volume of illness-causing bacteria and unpleasant odour to indoor air.

Other domestic culprits: fireplaces, odours and chemicals from hobbies like photography and model building, ceramic glazes, uncleaned carpets, oil paints, dusty closets, plastic shades, synthetic toys, mouldy/dusty wallpaper, room sprays, mosquito coils, cigarette smoke, cosmetics, nail care products, certain kinds of scented candles, smoke from extinguished candles, etc.

Smoke Is Damaging

Smoking leaves the air heavy with cancer-causing toxins. Even by smoking outside, toxins cling to clothes. Many are released in the indoor air. Most vulnerable are those confined to home: the sick, the elderly, pregnant women and babies.

Exposure to high indoor-smoke levels has been linked to pregnancy-related problems like stillbirths and low birth weight in studies in Latin America, Asia, and Africa. IAP has also been linked to blindness and immune-system depression. A recent WHO [World Health Organization] study found that over 2,000,000 children worldwide suffer from environmental hazards including IAP.

Studies by The Energy and Resources Institute (TERI), New Delhi, reveal that urbanites who work in ill-ventilated, air-conditioned buildings and offices are at risk, since this construction "may lead to sick-building syndrome". And slum

Major Health-Damaging Pollutants Generated from Indoor Sources

Pollutant	Major Indoor Sources
Fine particles	Fuel/tobacco combustion, cleaning operations, cooking
Carbon monoxide	Fuel/tobacco combustion
Polycyclic aromatic hydrocarbons	Fuel/tobacco combustion, cooking
Nitrogen oxides	Fuel combustion
Sulfur oxides	Coal combustion
Arsenic and fluorine	Coal combustion
Volatile and semi-volatile organic compounds	Fuel/tobacco combustion, consumer products, furnishings, construction materials, cooking
Aldehydes	Furnishing, construction materials, cooking
Pesticides	Consumer products, dust from outside
Asbestos	Remodeling/demolition of construction materials
Lead	Remodeling/demolition of painted surfaces
Biological pollutants	Moist areas, ventilation systems, furnishings
Radon	Soil under building, construction materials
Free radicals and other short-lived, highly reactive compounds	Indoor chemistry

TAKEN FROM: J. Zhang and K. R. Smith, "Indoor Air Pollution: A Global Health Concern," *British Medical Bulletin*, vol. 67, 2003.

dwellers are in double trouble. As TERI fellow R. Uma puts it, they use solid fuels, live in poorly ventilated homes, "facing the double burden of poor indoor as well as outdoor air pollution".

So, is anything being done about it? There is an ongoing study in India supported by the World Bank and the Energy Sector Management Assistance Program (ESMAP)— "Household Energy, [Indoor] Air Pollution, and Health".

As the World Bank report notes, combating IAP needs "awareness raising among government decision makers and (the public), and ... interventions in ... petroleum sector, small business development, improved stoves programmes, rural poverty alleviation strategies and health education." That sounds like a tall order but there is much that we can do.

What You Can Do

LPG [liquefied petroleum gas, or propane] and electricity are healthier for cooking. Modern fuels are especially needed in vulnerable rural areas. Keep kitchens scrupulously clean. Minimise cockroach/insect pollution by covering food, waste bins and drainage outlets. Avoid smoking, outdoors or indoors.

Dr. Paramesh's suggestions: Allow plenty of sunlight into the home (it kills germs, prevents fungi moulds) and permit cross ventilation. Sun mattresses, pillows, and carpets regularly. Ideal relative humidity for the home is 40 to 50 per cent. Air conditioners are good: They bring in fresh air and keep out the allergens. But the room's humidity levels should not go out of the ideal range. Clean the AC [air conditioner] unit's filters regularly. Ill-maintained ones have even been known to kill people, from the *Legionella* bacteria. Stuffed or fluffy toys collect dust easily: wooden toys with herbal dyes (lead causes IAP) are better. Pets are okay, if you keep them clean and, keep out of the home, the dangerous cat urine, dog and cat saliva and dandruff.

Indoor air purifiers are big business abroad but most experts say they are not suitable for Indian weather and construction conditions. A better (and cheaper) alternative is indoor plants, which absorb carbon dioxide and emit oxygen.

You can tell that immediately when you enter the office of Dr. S. Aswath, [joint] director of horticulture, Karnataka, whose office has a profusion of potted plants, terrariums, and an indoor landscaped garden with windows built to flood the room with sunlight and fresh air. The arrangement is not just of decorative value, he tells you: It purifies the air and even improves mood of people who come in.

You couldn't agree more as you inhale the pure, clean, almost therapeutic air in his room. Money plants, chrysanthemums (chrysanthemum received worldwide attention when NASA [National Aeronautics and Space Administration] found it was one of the best flowering plants for removing formaldehyde, benzene and ammonia from the atmosphere!) and bamboo plants (most effective) are good for combating IAP. Better than room sprays and colognes, which fill the air with chemicals.

Central and Southern Asia Deal with a Growing Number of Asthma Sufferers

Medical News Today

Medical News Today is an online health news service. In the following viewpoint, it reviews a new report on the increasing prevalence of asthma worldwide that states that more than 50 million people living in central and southern Asia suffer from the disease. The report also predicts that asthma rates will continue to climb because of urbanization and rapid industrialization in the region.

As you read, consider the following questions:

1. According to the report, the prevalence of asthma will increase most dramatically in what country?
2. What is the range of the prevalence of asthma in central and southern Asia?
3. How many people worldwide are affected by asthma, according to the viewpoint?

O ver 50 million people in central and southern Asia have asthma, and many do not have access to the medications that can control the disease, according to a report released to-

Medical News Today, "Over 50 Million Suffer from Asthma in Central and Southern Asia—Prevalence Predicted to Continue Increasing in Coming Years," May 13, 2007. Content from http://www.ginasthma.org used with permission from The Global Initiative for Asthma (GINA).

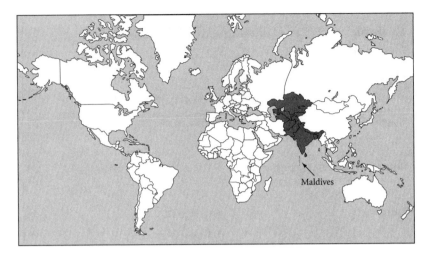

Maldives

day, World Asthma Day. The *Global Burden of Asthma* report, which details the prevalence, morbidity, and mortality of asthma in 20 regions around the world, reveals a number of alarming facts about the burden of this chronic respiratory disease in central and southern Asia.

Due to rapid industrialization and urbanization throughout the region, the prevalence of asthma is predicted to increase rapidly in the coming years. The increase is likely to be particularly dramatic in India, which is projected to become the world's most populous nation by 2050. An absolute 2% increase in the prevalence of asthma in India would result in an additional 20 million people with the disease.

> *Due to rapid industrialization and urbanization through-out the region, the prevalence of asthma is predicted to increase rapidly in the coming years.*

Asthma Rates in Region Have Jumped

The prevalence of asthma in central and southern Asia ranges from 1.5% in Nepal to 4.6% in Uzbekistan—relatively low compared to some other parts of the world. However, the

Examples of Agents Causing Asthma in Selected Occupations

Occupation/Occupational Field	Agent
	Animal and Plant Proteins
Bakers	Flour, amylase
Dairy farmers	Storage mites
Detergent manufacturing	*Bacillus subtilis* enzymes
Electrical soldering	Colophony (pine resin)
Farmers	Soybean dust
Fish food manufacturing	Midges, parasites
Food processing	Coffee bean dust, meat tenderizer, tea, shellfish, amylase, egg proteins, pancreatic enzymes, papain
Granary workers	Storage mites, *Aspergillus*, indoor ragweed, grass
Health care workers	Psyllium, latex
Laxative manufacturing	Ispaghula, psyllium
Poultry farmers	Poultry mites, droppings, feathers
Research workers, veterinarians	Locusts, dander, urine proteins
Sawmill workers, carpenters	Wood dust (western red cedar, oak, mahogany, zebrawood, redwood, Lebanon cedar, African maple, eastern white cedar)
Shipping workers	Grain dust (molds, insects, grain)
Silk workers	Silk worm moths and larvae
	Inorganic Chemicals
Beauticians	Persulfate
Plating	Nickel salts
Refinery workers	Platinum salts, vanadium

continued

Examples of Agents Causing Asthma in Selected Occupations [CONTINUED]

Occupation/Occupational Field	Agent
	Organic Chemicals
Automobile painting	Ethanolamine, dissocyanates
Hospital workers	Disinfectants (sulfathiazole, chloramines, formaldehyde, glutaraldehyde), latex
Manufacturing	Antibiotics, piperazine, methyldopa, salbutamol, cimetidine
Rubber processing	Formaldehyde, ethylene diamine, phthalic anhydride
Plastics industry	Toluene dissocyanate, hexamethyl dissocyanate, dephenylmethyl isocyanate, phthalic anhydride, triethylene tetramines, trimellitic anhydride, hexamethyl tetramine, acrylates

TAKEN FROM: "Global Strategy for Asthma Management and Prevention," *GINA*, 2008.

---

prevalence of asthma has increased markedly in recent years, with up to a threefold increase seen among children in southern Asia over the last two decades.

Asthma is a chronic lung disease characterized by recurrent breathing problems and symptoms such as breathlessness, wheezing, chest tightness, and coughing. Asthma symptoms vary over time, and also differ in severity from one individual to another. When it is not effectively treated, asthma often leads to hospitalization, missed work and school, limitations on physical activity, sleepless nights and in some cases death.

Although asthma cannot be cured, effective medications to treat and manage the disease exist. One of the authors of the *Global Burden of Asthma* report, Professor Richard Beasley, of the Medical Research Institute of New Zealand, says, "In central and southern Asia, effective asthma management is often limited by lack of availability or affordability of medications." In some areas widespread misconceptions about asthma and its treatment, and reluctance of patients to use the inhaler devices that are key to effective delivery of asthma medicines, also pose challenges. "Low-cost asthma education and management programs are needed to ensure that asthma care is available and affordable for all segments of the population in central and southern Asia," adds Professor Beasley.

Asthma is now one of the world's most common long-term conditions. . . . The disease is estimated to affect as many as 300 million people worldwide. . . .

The high levels of air pollution in central and southern Asia are also cause for concern. "The inhabitants of some Indian and Bangladeshi cities are exposed to some of the highest air pollution levels in the world," Professor Beasley says. "Air pollution can trigger asthma attacks, and can also worsen the symptoms of a variety of other respiratory diseases." Indoor air pollution, from burning biomass fuel for cooking and heating in poorly ventilated dwellings, also contributes to the burden of asthma and other respiratory diseases in the region.

The Prevalence of Asthma Worldwide

Asthma is now one of the world's most common long-term conditions, according to the *Global Burden of Asthma* report. The disease is estimated to affect as many as 300 million people worldwide—a number that could increase by a further 100 million by 2025.

The *Global Burden of Asthma* report is a comprehensive survey of the prevalence and impact of asthma around the world based on standardized data collected in epidemiology studies in more than 80 countries. This groundbreaking report has been written by Richard Beasley, Matthew Masoli, Denise Fabian, and Shaun Holt, of the Medical Research Institute of New Zealand and the University of Southampton in the UK [United Kingdom]. Initial results of the report were released on World Asthma Day 2003; the report is being released in full today.

The report was commissioned by the Global Initiative for Asthma (GINA), an effort launched in 1993 to work with health care professionals and public health officials around the world to reduce the burden of asthma. Guidelines for the diagnosis and management of asthma prepared by GINA have been adapted for use in a variety of settings around the world, illustrating how asthma management programs can be tailored to fit the local culture and level of resources available.

GINA also sponsors World Asthma Day, held each year on the first Tuesday in May. This event aims to raise awareness of asthma around the world and encourage individual countries to take urgent action and make asthma a major health priority within their own regions.

In the *Global Burden of Asthma* report, the region "Central Asia and Pakistan" includes the following countries: Afghanistan, Kazakhstan, Kyrgyzstan, Pakistan, Tajikistan, Turkmenistan, and Uzbekistan. The region "Southern Asia" includes: Bangladesh, Bhutan, India, Nepal, Seychelles, and Sri Lanka.

Canadian Statistics on Health Problems Caused by Air Pollution Are Problematic

Ross McKitrick

Ross McKitrick is a professor of economics at the University of Guelph. In the following viewpoint, he argues that statistical models used to estimate the number of Canadians who die from air pollution may be flawed. McKitrick believes that the number is much less than has been reported in previous studies.

As you read, consider the following questions:

1. According to Toronto Public Health, how many premature deaths from air pollution occur each year in Toronto?
2. How many hospitalizations occur each year in Toronto because of air pollution?
3. What does McKitrick identify as the fifth weakness in earlier statistical models?

For many years we have heard that air pollution in Canada is responsible for thousands of annual deaths and hospitalizations. In 2004 Toronto Public Health claimed that 1,700 premature deaths and 6,000 hospitalizations occur each year in Toronto alone, due to air pollution. The Ontario Medical

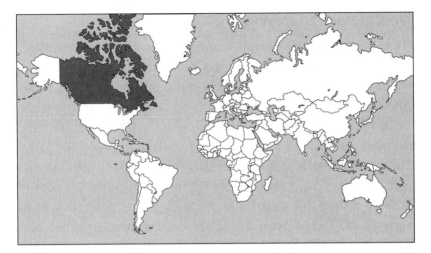

Association, provincial and federal governments, lung associations and other groups regularly cite these kinds of figures in support of calls for new regulatory initiatives. These death and hospitalization rates are astonishing. It is like suffering a 9/11-sized terrorist attack [referring to the September 11, 2001, terrorist attacks on the United States] every 10 months.

But is it really true? The estimates are derived by taking correlations in the epidemiological literature between observed pollution levels and health indicators, like hospital admission rates, and then extrapolating across populations to estimate how many deaths and illness diagnoses can, in theory, be attributed to pollution. In other words, the numbers come from statistical models, not from direct observations. That means we need to pay close attention to how the statistical modeling is done.

Together with my coauthors Gary Koop of Strathclyde University and Lise Tole of the University of Edinburgh, I have just published a peer-reviewed study in the journal *Environmental Modelling & Software* that does just that. What we found gives us reason to believe that the kind of statistical modeling behind common claims about air pollution may need a careful second look.

Weaknesses in Previous Studies

There are hundreds of studies in the epidemiological literature that have reported correlations between air pollution and health measures. But there are some common weaknesses to this literature. First, the results are not consistent across studies. Some studies find particulate matter (PM) affects health, but not sulphur dioxide (SO_2) or carbon monoxide (CO). Others reported SO_2 has an effect, but not PM. Another reports CO has an effect but not ozone (O_3), while another finds O_3 matters in some cities but not others. One large U.S. study found PM increased mortality risk a little bit across the U.S., except in 20 out of 88 cities in which it actually reduced mortality risk. These kinds of inconsistencies should not occur if the health effect is based on a real physiological response. This is a second puzzling aspect of the literature: Despite decades of testing, clinical investigations have not found experimental support for the idea that current ambient air pollution levels cause lung disease or mortality.

A third weakness of the literature is that studies tend to use short panels of data from recent years (post-1990) when air pollution levels were rather low and steady. When constructing a statistical model of the effect of an explanatory variable (such as the effect of PM levels on hospital admissions) it is difficult to identify the correlation if the explanatory variable does not change much over the sample. Use of short panels with low variation can lead to unstable parameter estimates.

A fourth weakness of the literature is that few studies control for important factors like smoking, income levels and weather. Some recent studies have added in socioeconomic covariates. After doing so, the apparent effect of pollution vanished.

A fifth weakness has to do with the fact that a researcher needs to make a great many choices about how to approach the data. There are dozens of variables that could potentially be included in the statistical model. The number of possible combinations can potentially run into the billions. How should a researcher choose which model to use? In many cases the decision is arbitrary: just pick one model and report the results. But in some cases when people have gone back and tried different models on the same data, they get different results. So it is important to use a methodology that takes into account the uncertainty associated with the fact that the researcher needs to choose how to construct the model and that the data will tend to support some models over others.

What we did not find was any evidence that increases in air pollution levels are associated with increased rates of hospital admissions.

A Reassessment of the Issue

Koop, Tole and I set out to re-examine the relationship between air pollution and health using a data set and methodology that would address these concerns. We were able to get a unique data set from Statistics Canada containing counts of hospital admissions for all lung-related ailments in 11 cities across the country from 1974 to 1994. This spans a time period when air pollution was initially higher than today, then steadily fell. If today's low air pollution sends thousands of people per year to the hospital in Toronto, then we should easily be able to identify the effect in previous years when pollution was double or triple its current concentrations. We then built a data set that included the urban air contaminants, average income, smoking rates, air temperature, wind speed and air pressure in each city over the same period. Finally, rather than picking one statistical model and relying on it, we used a technique called Bayesian model averaging that evaluates all possible model specifications, assesses the support each one gets in the data and then constructs parameter and uncertainty estimates based on the whole distribution.

We found, not surprisingly, that smoking is bad for lung health. We found that regions with higher gross domestic product (GDP) tend to have higher hospital admission rates, depending on the model specification, which may indicate that those regions have more hospital services. And we found evidence that hot days with high air pressure tend to produce more hospital admissions.

So the bottom line is that, for the purpose of assessing the link between air pollution levels and hospital admissions, one needs to look closely at the kinds of studies being done and how they did the statistical modeling.

No Supporting Evidence

What we did not find was any evidence that increases in air pollution levels are associated with increased rates of hospital admissions. We looked at the data every which way imaginable. If we were to cherry pick, by looking only at a subsample of the time or by picking just the right form of the model, we could find evidence that CO or nitrogen dioxide (NO_2) have positive effects on lung disease, but those results do not get strong support in the data. The models that get consistent support either show no pollution effects or—paradoxically— negative effects. In other words, in some cases as air pollution rises, hospital admissions go down. As odd as that sounds, we are by no means the first to report negative coefficients in the literature. Nobody is trying to argue that air pollution is good for you: This is either just noise in the data, or it might be an effect from "averting" behaviour, where people who are susceptible to lung problems stay indoors on days with bad air quality.

Based on our analysis, we could estimate what the effect on hospital admissions would be if all the pollution currently observed in Toronto air were to disappear. Toronto Public Health claims about 6,000 fewer hospitalizations would occur.

But this claim gets no support in the data. We found that there would be no reduction in lung-related hospitalizations. If anything there might be somewhere between 20 and 200 more admissions, if we apply the statistical results in a mechanical fashion.

Very few studies over the past decade have controlled for socioeconomic covariates (including smoking), fewer still have looked at long data panels back to the 1970s and fewer still have dealt with model uncertainty. Those that have addressed one or more of these issues typically find the effect of air pollution shrinks or disappears outright. Thus our results are actually quite consistent with the relevant group of previous studies. The popular idea that current ambient air pollution has a powerful effect on lung health might look like it is based on a large empirical foundation, but on closer inspection the pile contains a lot of weak results.

So the bottom line is that, for the purpose of assessing the link between air pollution levels and hospital admissions, one needs to look closely at the kinds of studies being done and how they did the statistical modeling. More studies need to be done using long time series that go back to the 1970s or earlier, more studies need to control for socioeconomic covariates and more studies need to take account of model uncertainty. Based on evidence to date, as these things begin to happen, we should not be surprised if current estimates of the health effects of air pollution turn out to be in need of major revision.

Mexico City Residents Suffer from a Loss of Smell from Chronic Air Pollution

Mica Rosenberg

Mica Rosenberg is a reporter for the international news agency Reuters. In the following viewpoint, Rosenberg announces that scientists claim the chronic air pollution that has affected Mexico City for years has worsened the residents' sense of smell. The unremitting air pollution has also resulted in higher rates of asthma and allergies as well as other health problems. (Additional reporting by Anahi Rama. Editing by Catherine Bremer.)

As you read, consider the following questions:

1. How many people live in Mexico City?

2. According to a 2007 study in the *American Journal of Respiratory and Critical Care Medicine,* what did scientists discover about Mexico City schoolchildren?

3. How many lives a year could be saved if there were a 10 percent drop in toxic air particles in Mexico City, according to the Blacksmith Institute?

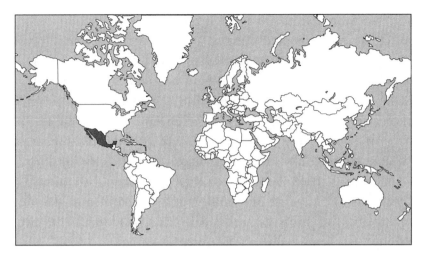

Mexico City (Reuters)—Chronic pollution in Mexico City, which stains the sky yellow and can trigger government warnings to stay indoors, could be killing off residents' sense of smell, scientists say.

Tests showed people in Mexico City—a sprawling metropolis crammed with around 20 million people and 4 million cars—struggled to sniff out everyday odors like coffee and orange juice compared to residents of a nearby town.

Mexico City is one of the world's most polluted capitals, along with Beijing, blighted by its thin high-altitude air and a ring of surrounding mountains that trap exhaust fumes belched from smoky buses and factories on the city outskirts.

Their noses are so badly damaged from a life inhaling toxic particles that they also find it harder to detect the scent of rotten food, said researcher Robyn Hudson who ran the study.

"We added a substance (to powdered milk) that is a common contaminant of food, something that smells disgusting basically—like a sour, rotting cabbage," said Hudson.

"We were able to see at what point . . . they would start to reject the contaminated sample, say 'ew yuck! no! take it away please,'" said Hudson, an Australian and a senior research scientist at Mexico's National Autonomous University (UNAM).

Mexico City is one of the world's most polluted capitals, along with Beijing, blighted by its thin high-altitude air and a ring of surrounding mountains that trap exhaust fumes belched from smoky buses and factories on the city outskirts.

Contamination levels are better now than two decades ago, but from a high-story window it's still hard most days to make out the snow-capped peaks that surround the city through the murky shroud of brownish smog.

Mexico City's ozone levels exceed World Health Organization standards on approximately 300 days of the year.

Vulnerable Cells

Hudson's team compared Mexico City dwellers with a group from the nearby rural state of Tlaxcala, and found country folk could detect contaminants at lower concentrations.

The researchers are now testing to see whether pollution can cause more serious cellular damage in the nose and eyes.

On entering the nose, odors pass through a thin layer of mucus where they are detected by sensory cells that send the brain messages that something reeks or smells rosy. The cells are vulnerable to damage from pollutants, Hudson said.

"The olfactory receptors are very exposed," she said. "They are just hanging out there in the mucus."

Hudson suspects pollution could also affect taste, given the two senses are intimately linked.

The loss of smell is one of a gamut of problems caused by Mexico City's smog, which prompts a handful of warnings a year for residents to avoid exercising or hanging about outside.

Health experts worry about lung infections, asthma, heart attacks and cancers. A 2007 study in the *American Journal of*

Respiratory and Critical Care Medicine found Mexico City schoolchildren had unusually small lungs.

The problem is aggravated by the fact Mexico City stands some 7,400 feet above sea level in a sunken lake bed rimmed by mountains. Its thin atmosphere and bowl-shaped valley concentrates pollutants within the city.

City authorities have worked to remove the worst-polluting vehicles from the road, but as the capital's population grows it buys up to 250,000 new cars each year.

Asthma, allergies and other respiratory problems are common among residents, whose grimy windows need weekly scraping.

A 10 percent drop in toxic air particles could save 3,000 lives a year and prevent 10,000 cases of chronic bronchitis, says pollution watchdog the Blacksmith Institute.

"I know I'm inhaling poison," said 38-year-old Guadalupe, a candy seller at a busy Mexico City road intersection with cars whizzing by. "But there is nothing I can do."

Periodical and Internet Sources Bibliography

The following articles have been selected to supplement the diverse views presented in this chapter.

Mustafa Abubakar	"Air Pollution Kills 2 Million Annually," *Daily Trust* (Nigeria), May 13, 2010.
Boimah J.V. Boimah	"'Then the Whole of Liberia Is Polluted,'" *New Democrat* (Liberia), June 18, 2010.
Daily Independent (Lagos)	"Coping with Fumes, Noise Pollution in Lagos," August 9, 2010.
Daily Nation (Kenya)	"Kenya: Health One of the Biggest Headaches for Slum Dwellers," April 6, 2010.
Christine Demsteader	"Underground Air 'Damages Stockholmers' Lungs,'" *Local* (Sweden), January 5, 2005.
Kate Kelland	"Few Chernobyl Radiation Risks from Russia Fires," *Kyiv Post* (Ukraine), August 11, 2010.
Rachel Myers Lowe	"Does Pollution Really Increase Stroke Risk?" *Calgary Herald* (Canada), July 9, 2010.
Amy Norton	"Living Near Traffic Pollution Tied to Heart Deaths," *China Daily*, July 16, 2010.
Nick O'Malley	"Panel to Focus on Coalmine Pollution," *Sydney Morning Herald*, April 22, 2010.
Julie Robotham	"Asthma Linked to Particles in Air Pollution," *Sydney Morning Herald*, March 22, 2010.
Helena Selby	"Ghana: Air Pollution—A Health Hazard to the Environment," *Chronicle* (Ghana), June 16, 2010.
Mike Tuffrey	"Poor Air Quality Is One of Britain's Biggest Health Issues," *Guardian* (UK), June 24, 2010.

GLOBALVIEWPOINTS

CHAPTER 3

The Political and Economical Effects of Air Pollution Policy

China Is Suspicious of Western Environmental Motives

Yu Zheng

Yu Zheng is a writer with the Xinhua News Agency. In the following viewpoint, Zheng contends that Western nations use environmental advocacy to maneuver themselves economically to maintain competitiveness in a world market. Zheng argues that China is doing quite well in transitioning to a greener economy in relation to its Western colleagues.

As you read, consider the following questions:

1. What did the Chinese president pledge to cut by 2020?
2. How many countries signed and approved the United Nations Framework Convention on Climate Change (UNFCCC)?
3. What ancient philosophy does the author state the Chinese people still abide by?

I keep coughing after a brief visit to a sizable developing nation—not because of a possible A(H1N1) infection but the continuous exposure to strong smell of fuel and pollutants on roads of the country, where 20-year-old obsolete cars rattled everywhere.

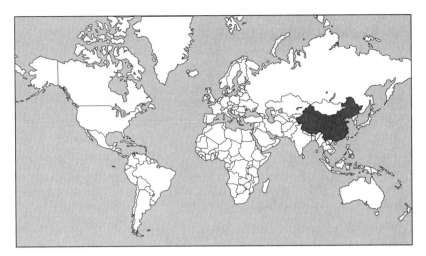

Coincidentally, a colleague of mine talked to me about one mountainous country he lately toured, saying that air pollution there was roughly 10 times, though he failed to supply scientific data, of that in Beijing.

China Is Implementing Green Technology

While many Beijing residents, including foreign expatriates, are still not satisfied with air quality in the city, the government of the Chinese capital is implementing one of the world's harshest vehicle emissions rules, particularly after 2008 when Beijing hosted a summer Olympics. The improvement is noticeable.

After three decades' rapid economic growth, China became the world's third largest economy as well as one of the biggest emitters of greenhouse gases (GHGs).

As almost all industrialized countries did in their early stages of development, China used to follow the growth path of ineffective energy consumption and rampant encroachment of natural resources.

Now China is eager to create a greener economy, for not only its own people, but also the whole planet. The Chinese

World's Most Polluted Cities

City	Country	PM10 (particulate matter less than 10 microns in diameter)
Cairo	Egypt	169
Delhi	India	150
Kolkata	India	128
Tianjin	China	125
Chongqing	China	123
Kanpur	India	109
Lucknow	India	109
Jakarta	Indonesia	104
Shenyang	China	101
Zhengzhou	China	97
Jinan	China	94
Lanzhou	China	91
Beijing	China	89
Taiyuan	China	88

TAKEN FROM: World Bank, "Beijing Pollution: Facts and Figures," BBC News, August 11, 2008. http://news.bbc.co.uk.

president pledged a marginal cut of GHGs emissions by 2020, even though no existing international conventions or regimes require China, as one developing nation, to make such a promise.

If we could only turn back time to the first decades of the global industrialization, China would have been ranked among the most self-disciplined students in the class due to the introspection of coordinating its own economic development with the needs for protecting nature. The United Nations Framework Convention on Climate Change (UNFCCC), which was signed and approved by more than 192 countries in the world, specifies that industrialized countries contributed to the biggest chunk of human emissions in history.

The Hypocrisy of the West

If there is any cap for each country in accordance with its historical performance, some scientists argue, all UNFCCC-annexed industrialized economies have already used up their respective portions of GHG emissions. Nonetheless, few UNFCCC-annexed developed countries are able to offer any meaningful emission cut plans close to their promises signed a dozen years ago into the Kyoto Protocol [an agreement of nations that is aimed at fighting global warming], which was under the UNFCCC regime. A lot of people in the wealthiest countries continue their proud lifestyle of living in big houses, driving gas-guzzling SUVs [sport-utility vehicles], and using highly powered washing machines and dryers. Short of mentioning the UNFCCC principle of "common but differentiated responsibilities" for sharing burdens of emissions cut, many industrialized nations are now shunning their responsibilities and asking developing members of the international community to make overdue contributions.

Not at all cynical of serious concern of climate change and global warming, Chinese should be aware of intentional control of wealth distribution under the pretext of lofty ideas.

How can those industrialized countries, which owe huge carbon debts to the world, occupy the moral beacon of achieving a greener and better world?

An unspoken intention is looming behind the moral advocacy in international climate talks. Powers which set up game rules would often refresh such rules to keep their competitiveness, in financial interests, social benefits and, consequently, national strength—from the Bretton Woods system which established the International Monetary Fund and the World Bank, to the consolidation of the World Trade Organization, and to the cap-and-trade mechanism these days and possibly global carbon exchange markets in the future. It's quite a cutting-edge gizmo to let carbon be a priced commodity, particularly after Wall Street met an unavoidable failure in securitizing everything, company stocks, life insurances and even bad debts. Just commercializing everything—climate, this time. Not at all cynical of serious concern of climate change and global warming, Chinese should be aware of intentional control of wealth distribution under the pretext of lofty ideas.

While enjoying the better-off after diligent and entrepreneurial work, the Chinese people still abide by the appeal of the ancient sage Lao Tzu, stay in harmony with the universe.

Iceland's Erupting Volcano Reflects Political and Economic Strife

Alda Sigmundsdóttir

Alda Sigmundsdóttir is a writer and translator. In the following viewpoint, she maintains that the eruption of the Eyjafjallajökull glacier in Iceland can be viewed as an allegory for the rage and frustration of the Icelandic people in the wake of the country's devastating economic collapse. Sigmundsdóttir speculates that the corrupt speculators and moguls who contributed to the collapse are grateful that the glacier has taken publicity away from reports of their wrongdoings.

As you read, consider the following questions:

1. According to the author, why is Thor Björgólfsson such a figure of controversy in Iceland?
2. The Kitchenware Revolution is the 2009 Icelandic financial crisis protests. How does that figure in the author's argument?
3. What does the author believe may be "Iceland's revenge"?

The news that an eruption had started in Eyjafjallajökull glacier, south Iceland, and that it was 10–30 times bigger than the eruption that started in a similar location three weeks

Alda Sigmundsdóttir, "Iceland's Rage at Bankers Is Yet to Erupt," *The Guardian* (UK), April 15, 2010. Copyright © Guardian News & Media Ltd. 2010. Reproduced by permission.

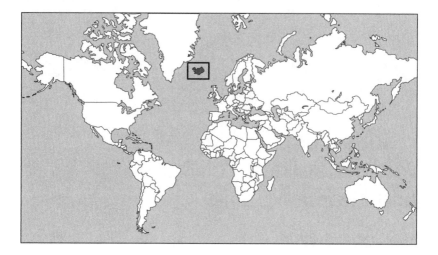

ago . . . well, it took a moment to sink in. Here, in Iceland, we were in the midst of the fallout from a fact-finding report into the bank collapse that had been published two days earlier—widely dubbed the "black report", on account of its staggering revelations of corruption and incompetence in the lead-up to the economic meltdown. The media was already working over-time to plough through the 2,000-plus-page report to offer up choice morsels for the public, which was already feeling com-pletely overwhelmed by its revelations.

When the media started reporting the news, the Icelandic blogosphere—an unfailing barometer of the national psyche—was already abuzz with indignation over an article that had appeared in one of the Icelandic papers that morning. It had been sent in by Thor Björgólfsson, former mogul and owner of Landsbanki—purveyor of the ill-fated Icesave banking ac-counts—and it was entitled "I apologise." In the article, Björgólfsson issued about five maudlin "apologies", while at the same time explaining why he was really not to blame and dropping choice phrases like:

> "Every Icelander is responsible for their finances and the de-cisions they took. I am no exception."

This from an individual who, it is revealed in the report, looked upon Landsbanki as a "smorgasbord" and, among other things, vacuumed hundreds of billions of Icelandic krónur out of it for his own purposes a mere month before the collapse.

There is, come to think of it, a sort of poetic allegory inherent in this new [volcanic] eruption.

So, it is easy to believe that folks like Thor Björgólfsson breathed a sigh of relief at the news that Eyjafjallajökull glacier had blown up—just in time to stop the lynching in the blogosphere and elsewhere.

There is, come to think of it, a sort of poetic allegory inherent in this new eruption. One could even view it as the symbolic rage of the collective Icelandic nation bursting forth—rage that has been seething beneath the surface of this apparently placid society ever since the so-called Kitchenware Revolution ended last year. Indeed, Icelandic riot police were standing by in case of potential civil unrest following the publication of the black report, which had been awaited with great anticipation, and which had already been delayed three times due to the scope of the investigation. Protests had even started on Monday outside the parliament buildings, but those, too, have apparently been diverted by news of the eruption.

And now, with flights grounded in the UK and northern Europe due to volcanic ash, it was predictable that the phrase "Iceland's revenge" would fly—suggesting that this was Iceland's payback to the United Kingdom for using anti-terrorist legislation to seize Icelandic assets after the bank collapse, and for playing serious hardball in the Icesave dispute. However, all such remarks that I have heard have come not from Icelanders, but from foreigners. Indeed, I believe the diplomatic dispute with the UK and the Netherlands over the Icesave affair is such a sensitive issue for most Icelanders that most would not even consider joking about it in such a flippant manner.

When Volcanic Ash Reaches the Ground

If the ash reaches the ground due to vertical movement of air masses, there is a risk of increased air pollution levels, notably of concentrations of respirable [capable of being taken in during breathing] particulate matter . . . , and of related health effects. This increase in pollution is expected to be small and in the range observed even without volcanic ash. It is normally caused by fluctuations in traffic or other human activities, and depends on weather conditions and the long-range transport of air pollution.

Daily fluctuations in particle concentrations may lead to changes in daily mortality rates and in the number of people being admitted to hospital for treatment of heart or lung disorders.

World Health Organization,
"Air Quality: Important Questions Answered on the Health
Effects of Volcanic Ash," May 21, 2010. www.euro.who.int.

Besides, we have other things to worry about. One bridge has already been washed out, the ring road that connects west and east Iceland on the south coast is severely damaged (and closed), farms are at risk, and the nearby Katla—a nasty volcano that could make this current eruption look like a walk in the park—could potentially be awakened. And as if that wasn't enough, we now face the wrath of irate UK tourists who can't get to their holiday destinations.

But it's an ill wind bearing volcanic ash that blows nobody any good, as they say: no doubt, the oligarchs and others implicated in the fact-finding report are enjoying this brief respite from the wrath that will surely rain down upon them in due course.

China's Explosive Growth Leads to Environmental Challenges

Jonathan Watts and Randeep Ramesh

Jonathan Watts is the Asia environmental correspondent and Randeep Ramesh is the social affairs editor for the Guardian, *a British national daily newspaper. In the following viewpoint, they argue that both China and India have suffered from the environmental consequences of rapid industrial growth over the past several years. Watts and Ramesh find that action to address these environmental problems has been complicated, although small signs of progress are evident.*

As you read, consider the following questions:

1. What Chinese city has been the most polluted place on the planet for the past five years?
2. How many people live in India and China?
3. Where is the world's biggest wind farm site being built?

In the most polluted city on earth, the smog is so thick that it seems to consume its source. Iron foundries, smelting plants and cement factories loom out of the haze then disappear once more as you drive along Linfen's roads. The out-

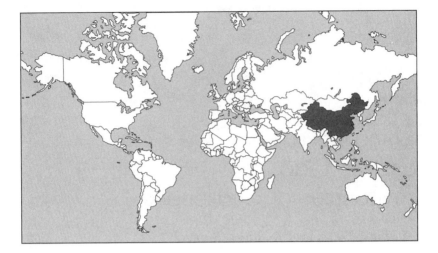

lines of smoke stacks blur in the filthy mist. No sooner are the plumes of carbon and sulphur belched out than the chimneys are swallowed up again.

"We only see the sun for a few days each year," said Zhou Huocun, a doctor in the outlying village of Liucunzhen. "The colour of our village is black. It is so dirty that nobody airs their quilts outside anymore so we are getting more parasites. I have seen a steady increase in respiratory diseases as the air quality gets worse and worse."

Outside Dr Zhou's hospital, shoes leave marks in the black dust. But it is a different type of carbon footprint that is drawing international attention to this part of the world.

Linfen is the front line of the battle against global warming. For the past five years, the city of 3.5 million people has been the most polluted place on the planet, bottom of the World Bank's air quality rankings, and a symbol of the worst side effects of China's breakneck economic growth.

Enveloped by a spectral haze, the city lies at the heart of a 12-mile industrial belt, fed by the 50m tonnes of coal mined each year in the nearby hills of Shanxi Province. The New York-based Blacksmith Institute puts it alongside Chernobyl on a list of the planet's 10 most contaminated places.

What Linfen symbolises is the cost of development in China and the other most populous country: India. Both economies are growing explosively, leading to a rapid expansion of their middle classes. This in turn has seen a growing appetite for power—one sated by the building of dirty, inefficient coal-fired plants that are slowly cooking the world's atmosphere.

The effects have been dramatic. By 2009 China is predicted to overtake the United States as the world's biggest emitter of greenhouse gases. India has recently become the fourth biggest polluter, but its steeply rising emissions will see it in third place within a few years.

China's three decades of industrial blitzkrieg has extracted a heavy price. Seventy percent of its rivers are contaminated. In the southern Himalayas, ancient glaciers are melting. Further north, encroaching deserts threaten the livelihoods of 400 million people.

By 2009 China is predicted to overtake the United States as the world's biggest emitter of greenhouse gases.

India, which is only half as rich as China, has also suffered. The frequency of catastrophic weather events such as flash flooding, say Indian meteorologists, is increasing. Clouds of brown soot cover the skies above the Indian Ocean for months each year. Agricultural scientists in the subcontinent note rising temperatures caused wheat yields to drop by a 10th last year.

The new consumption culture has brought Western-style affluence that largely rural India can barely cope with. Car sales are growing at 20% a year, but there are not enough roads for anyone to drive on. India—unlike China, Europe and America—does not set any fuel economy standards.

The result is that in the backstreets of a city such as Kanpur on the banks of the Ganges sit lines of cars, their engines idling in the sun. Kanpur, with 3 million people, is the world's seventh most polluted place, according to the World Bank study. A thick brown haze of exhaust fumes is visible at street level.

Last year the *Guardian* found hundreds of people queuing outside the government hospital, their mouths covered with dirty rags. "About 40% of the patients coming with respiratory diseases are affected by the atmospheric pollution," said Dr R P Singh, who describes the air as a "killer".

The environmental problems in India and China, which between them have 2.4 billion people, have become an excuse for inaction elsewhere. Many Britons argue that whatever positive steps they take will be insignificant compared with the negative impact of economic growth in Asia. As Tony Blair puts it: "Close down all of Britain's emissions and in less than two years just the growth in China's emissions would wipe out the difference."

British officials on a visit to Delhi this year told the *Guardian* that they were sceptical that India and China would sacrifice growth for green measures. "They are talking about climate change but doing very little in reality," said a source.

But for those seeking good news, it can be found even in China. Linfen is trying to clean up. By the end of this year, the city aims to close 160 of 196 iron foundries, and 57 of 153 coking plants. By replacing small, dirty and dangerous plants with large, cleaner and more carefully regulated facilities, the local government in Linfen plans to drastically reduce emissions. Central heating will be provided by gas instead of coal.

The changes are being driven by business (nobody wants to invest in such a polluted place), bureaucratic self-interest (local officials find it difficult to be promoted) and shifting political priorities.

"We have more power than before," said Yang Zhaofen, director of Linfen's environmental bureau. "The mayor says we can sacrifice economic growth in order to improve air quality. That used to be unthinkable."

There are already small signs of change. Last year, Linfen's residents breathed 163 days of unhealthy air, 15 days fewer than in 2005. Many factories have already been closed—not a wisp of smoke emerges from their chimneys. Thanks partly to such measures, Linfen lost its bottom spot in China's latest pollution rankings to the far-flung western city of Urumqi.

Blame

Both Beijing and New Delhi argue that they must use more energy to lift their populations from poverty, and that emissions per person are a fraction of those in rich states. Manmohan Singh, the Indian prime minister, told a conference this month: "The principal polluters are the United States and countries of western Europe. Per capita emissions are far ahead [of India and China]. You cannot preserve energy by perpetuating poverty in the poor nations."

The figures bear out his words. India emits 1.1 tonnes of carbon dioxide per person. China puts out 3.5 tonnes. Both are less than the global average of 4.2 tonnes. The comparable figures for the UK and America are 9.6 and 20.2 tonnes respectively.

Last year the Indian president, Abdul Kalam, a former scientist, called for 25% of power generation to come from renewable sources by 2030. The figure is now just 6%.

Both Beijing and New Delhi argue that they must use more energy to lift their populations from poverty, and that emissions per person are a fraction of those in rich states.

The country, which started its renewables ministry a decade ago, is building the world's biggest wind farm site, with 500 turbines outside Mumbai. The farm will have a capacity of 1,000MW.

Change in Emissions Intensity for Top 25 Emitters, 1992–2006

China	−36.9%
U.S.	−24.6%
Russia	−34.0%
India	−22.2%
Japan	−7.3%
Brazil	+6.9%
Germany	−23.4%
Canada	−21.8%
United Kingdom	−34.5%
Mexico	−7.7%
Indonesia	+17.8%
South Korea	−17.5%
Italy	−6.8%
Australia	−11.0%
Iran	+16.2%
France	−22.1%
Ukraine	−31.7%
Spain	−3.8%
South Africa	−12.9%
Turkey	−1.8%
Saudi Arabia	+17.5%
Poland	−51.1%
Thailand	+24.6%
Argentina	−8.9%
Nigeria	−39.0%

Top 25 emitters based on 2005 total GHG emissions estimates (excluding land-use change and forestry and international bunker fuels).

TAKEN FROM: World Bank 2009/World Resources Institute, "Emissions Intensity," *Climate Analysis Indicators Tool,* 2009. http://cait.wri.org.

"We are helping to make India one of only four countries in the world that can manufacture and export such technologies," said Tulsi Tanti, founder and managing director of Suzlon, which is building the wind farm. "Global warming created a great awareness for us. We have the support of the government and with the economy growing by 8–10% there will be a power deficit which we can fill with clean wind power."

In China there's also a growing appreciation of the unsustainable nature of red-hot economic growth, which has led to new green policies. In an address to the National People's Congress this month, the Chinese prime minister, Wen Jiabao, promised that "backward" factories would be shut down and energy efficiency improved to "bring pollution under control and protect the environment".

Previous leaders have failed to keep similar pledges. Mr Wen acknowledged that China had fallen short of its environmental targets last year. According to the latest five-year plan, China should use 20% less energy per unit of economic output by 2010. Last year, however, it managed to improve energy efficiency by only 1%.

Yang Ailun, climate campaigner for Greenpeace in China, said the country was slowly waking up to environmental problems, but not necessarily in terms of greenhouse gas emissions. "They are worried about the immediate causes of pollution—like river contamination—rather than global warming. Climate change seems far away," she said. "If the government is really serious about environmental protection, then we need to change our economic structure and reduce our dependency on coal."

The timing is critical. The Kyoto Protocol, which required developed countries to reduce their emissions by 5% from 1990 levels, expires in 2012. China and India were not given targets under the Kyoto Protocol while America refused to ratify it. The upshot is that none of these three giants have any binding commitment to cut emissions.

But for an effective replacement for the protocol, these three will have to take part in negotiations by 2010. Much depends on the US, which is responsible for about a quarter of all emissions. Without willing American engagement, the chances of a new agreement are small.

Unequivocal

Rajendra Pachauri, chairman of the UN Intergovernmental Panel on Climate Change, which last month reported that global warming was "unequivocal" and caused by human activity, said the only reasonable solution was to cut emissions of greenhouse gases gradually, while attempting to find new, low-carbon, energy sources, such as wind, solar, water and nuclear power.

"But we cannot ask developing countries like India and China to bear all of this burden. Both have a point when they say that all the carbon dioxide was emitted in the process of the West becoming industrialised especially by the United States," Dr Pachauri said. "India and China will argue that this is not a problem created by themselves."

"Instead we will find that people in the West will have to change their behaviour and conserve energy, use less power, perhaps wear warmer clothes in cold winters rather than turning up the central heating. It also means countries like India will need help building railways so that their public transport systems can cope with the growth."

When negotiations start this December for a deal to replace the Kyoto Protocol, China and India will resist binding targets to reduce emissions. New Delhi will probably seek technology to reduce carbon emissions from its power plants. At most, Beijing might agree to goals on energy efficiency and greater use of alternatives to coal and oil.

Shame could prove the great motivator. "The whole world will soon say to China, 'You are the number one emitter. You have got to do something,'" said Jeffrey Sachs, head of the Earth Institute at Columbia University. Speaking at a recent lecture in Beijing, Professor Sachs said China needed to move quickly towards clean coal and carbon capture technology.

"The safe use of fossil fuels is the single most important source of hope in China and India."

Kuwait Formulates a Plan to Alleviate Air Pollution Problems

Nawara Fattahova

Nawara Fattahova is a staff writer for the Kuwait Times. *In the following viewpoint, Fattahova outlines the accusations of environmentalists against the Kuwaiti Environment Public Authority (EPA) involving corruption and negligence. The EPA's poor performance, environmentalists charge, results in worsening health problems for the Kuwaiti people.*

As you read, consider the following questions:

1. What is the Green Line Environmental Society (GLES)?
2. To whose attention did GLES bring the numerous environmental violations they found?
3. According to GLES, what happened in the Kuwaiti suburb of Salmiya?

Kuwait's environment is in danger and the government is not taking the necessary measures to protect it. As many violations are occurring in the environmental field, the Green Line Environmental Society (GLES) is watching the Kuwaiti environment and is trying to help preserve and protect it. GLES, a voluntary NGO [nongovernmental organization], recently detected serious and dangerous environmental violations. The society has reported the matter to the concerned

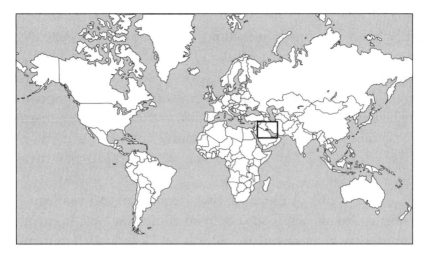

authorities responsible for the environment—the Environment Public Authority (EPA)—but they have not received any response until now.

GLES decided to bring the matter up with His Highness the Prime Minister Sheikh Nasser Al-Mohammed Al-Sabah. "Kuwait should be rescued from environmental crimes committed against its residents which are caused by the negligence of the EPA. I call upon the Prime Minister Sheikh Nasser Al-Mohammed to use his authority to solve these problems. We demand an independent committee be formed so we can investigate the reasons behind the corruption spreading in the EPA. The investigation should last for three months so the committee could issue a detailed report about the poor performance of the EPA and its participation on environmental crimes and violations. The report should also give solutions and recommendations," said GLES Chairman Khalid Al-Hajri.

EPA Has Been Negligent

Al-Hajri pointed out that the EPA was very negligent of its duties. "EPA is hiding relevant information from the public in order to distance the Kuwaiti society from Kuwait's environmental reality. GLES demanded for various types of environmental information from the EPA, but they never replied as they know that this information would be added to the environmental report which will be submitted to the Parliament," he added.

The EPA is committing further crimes and violations. "The EPA approved of the actions of a company to inject dangerous kinds of poisonous chemical waste in the earth. If GLES didn't interfere and stop this company, Kuwait's environment would have been destroyed," Al-Hajri pointed out.

Salmiya, one of the most vital commercial and residential areas in Kuwait, was a subject of corruption as well. "Cement factories, which spread poisonous and carcinogen cement dust, were allowed to be built in Salmiya's residential area. The EPA didn't move a muscle to sanction these factories and this led GLES to hold a campaign demanding the closure of these factories. Fortunately our campaign was successful and the factories were closed," Al-Hajri further said.

Kuwait's environment is in danger and the government is not taking the necessary measures to protect it.

Children Are Victims

He further noted that children living in Kuwait's southern areas are suffering from different diseases. "The southern areas, especially Umm Al-Haiman has become a storage area of diseases caused by the spread of poisonous gases. The air pollution detecting department at the EPA didn't even react on the calls for aid from the residents there," Al-Hajri explained.

GLES managed to get a document issued by the US Army, which proves that gas pollution percentages have been extremely high in Shuaiba industrial area for four years already. "The EPA knows about this, but they still haven't done anything to fix this problem. We haven't seen any positive changes," highlighted Al-Hajri.

Other areas are suffering from pollution as well. "Many residential areas that are located next to industrial areas are suffering from pollution. For instance, Shuwaikh industrial area is full of environmental violations and many chemical materials are stored there. This is like a bomb that could explode at any minute," he added.

Dump Sites and Marine Life

According to Al-Hajri, the EPA is useless in many other fields and areas. "The EPA has also failed to effectively help in rescuing Kuwait's marine environment, which is the State's main resource of water and fish. The marine pollution has even spread to numerous Kuwaiti islands," he noted.

Dump sites are a critical and dangerous problem in Kuwait as well. "Kuwait is now full of dump sites due to the negligence of the EPA, given that it has not implemented a plan for recycling waste. Dangerous gases are being produced since there are so many dump sites. Furthermore, these gasses could explode at any moment given that these gasses contain methane gas. The best example of this problem is the Qurain dump site, which hasn't been solved since 1979," Al-Hajri concluded.

Europe Worries That Cleaner Air Accelerates Climate Change

Volker Mrasek

Volker Mrasek is a contributor to German newsweekly Der Spiegel. *In the following viewpoint, he reports that scientists believe that antipollution policies in Europe have had the unintended consequences of accelerating climate change, because there are less particulates in the air to filter out harmful sunlight.*

As you read, consider the following questions:

1. How much has the average surface air temperature between the Bosporus and the Bay of Biscay risen since 1980?
2. According to the author, how do sulfates work on sunlight?
3. According to the German Meteorological Society, what will be the median temperature in Europe in 2040 in relation to that right before the Industrial Revolution?

The 1970s were a hazy time: Cars ran on sulfur-rich gasoline, power plants and heavy industry burned sulfur-rich coal. Europe lay under a blanket of fumes filled with sulphate particles. Acid rain brought the particles back to earth, ravaging the continent's forests.

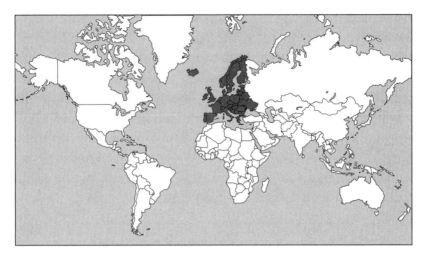

Air Pollution in Europe Today

That was then. The situation today is considerably different. Auto emissions are low in sulfur, power plants only run with smoke filters and acid rain is no longer an issue. But the success of efforts to restore Europe's air quality have had an unintended side effect that is just now coming to light. Because the atmosphere over Europe is increasingly clean, global warming is impacting the continent more quickly than other regions of the world.

The dwindling clouds of pollution are apparently the reason that Europe is heating faster than other mid-latitude regions. Since 1980, the average surface air temperature between the Bosporus [a strait that forms a boundary between Europe and Asia] and the Bay of Biscay has risen by almost an entire degree Celsius—twice as much as expected. The reasons for this were until recently a matter of heated dispute. Greenhouse gases could explain half that increase, at best. But now climate researchers in Germany, Switzerland and the United States, using data and computer simulations, claim that the rise in temperatures has been caused most directly by a decline in sulfate aerosols in the atmosphere.

Sulfates work like a filter on sunlight: They reflect short-wave solar radiation back into space, thereby letting less energy pass into the layer of air closest to the ground. But because the concentration of sulfur particles is declining so rapidly, this unintended cooling effect no longer works the way it once did—and Europe is getting hotter. To Martin Wild of the Swiss Federal Institute of Technology Zurich (ETH Zurich), it makes perfect sense: "We have less aerosol in the atmosphere, more radiation reaching the surface of the earth and an exorbitant increase in temperature."

Because the atmosphere over Europe is increasingly clean, global warming is impacting the continent more quickly than other regions of the world.

At the annual conference of the European Geosciences Union (EGU), which begins on Tuesday [in April 2008] in Vienna, climatologists and atmospheric researchers will discuss whether the trend will continue. As the air in developing regions like India and central Africa get ever dirtier and the light penetrating the cloud of pollution dims, Europe is rapidly getting brighter.

A Major Shift

Together with Joel Norris, an atmospheric scientist at the Scripps Institution of Oceanography in San Diego, Wild has been calculating fluctuations in European radiation levels. In the middle of the 1980s, there appears to have been a major shift. Until then, as the air became its most sulfur-laden, radiation near the surface reached all-time lows of around three watts per square meter. Beginning in 1986, when efforts to clean the air began to pay off and the atmosphere became more transparent to sunlight, radiation started to increase about 2 watts per square meter in each year over the next decade.

Wild based his work on an aerosol-tracking computer simulation developed by researchers at the Max Planck Institute for Meteorology in Hamburg. "Extensive air pollution temporarily compensated for the global warming in Europe," said Johann Feichter, leader of the institute's Aerosol, Clouds and Climate working group.

Sulfate particles not only minimize the transfer of solar radiation directly, they also encourage the accumulation of water droplets and clouds in the atmosphere—which in turn creates a second, indirect form of radiation repellent, because the light-colored surface of clouds reflects sunlight. This is where it gets complicated, though. In the landmark report issued last year [2007] by the Intergovernmental Panel on Climate Change (IPCC), the United Nations organization stated that questions persist about the effect that sulfate aerosols have on the atmosphere.

"Our findings contradict the IPCC," said Rolf Philipona of MeteoSwiss, Switzerland's national weather service. He and his colleague Christian Ruckstuhl, who now works as a researcher in California, analyzed data from 25 weather stations in northern Germany and eight in Switzerland.

"We found that the increase in radiation on the ground is considerably greater under a cloudless sky than a clouded one," Philipona told *Spiegel Online*. The direct impact of particulate pollution is about five times greater than the indirect impact, he explained. That shows, he claims, that sulfate aerosols play "a truly important, immediate role" in Europe's climate conditions.

Europe's air is not likely to get much cleaner than it is now—neither in summer nor in winter.

Cleaner Air and Climate Change

Geert Jan van Oldenborgh agrees. A physicist from the Royal [Netherlands] Meteorological Institute (KNMI), van Olden-

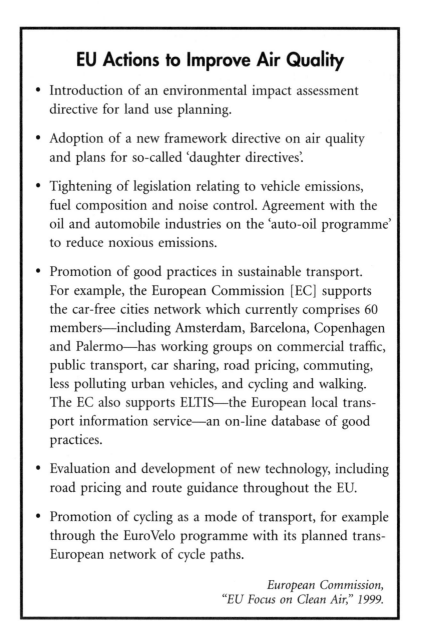

EU Actions to Improve Air Quality

- Introduction of an environmental impact assessment directive for land use planning.

- Adoption of a new framework directive on air quality and plans for so-called 'daughter directives'.

- Tightening of legislation relating to vehicle emissions, fuel composition and noise control. Agreement with the oil and automobile industries on the 'auto-oil programme' to reduce noxious emissions.

- Promotion of good practices in sustainable transport. For example, the European Commission [EC] supports the car-free cities network which currently comprises 60 members—including Amsterdam, Barcelona, Copenhagen and Palermo—has working groups on commercial traffic, public transport, car sharing, road pricing, commuting, less polluting urban vehicles, and cycling and walking. The EC also supports ELTIS—the European local transport information service—an on-line database of good practices.

- Evaluation and development of new technology, including road pricing and route guidance throughout the EU.

- Promotion of cycling as a mode of transport, for example through the EuroVelo programme with its planned trans-European network of cycle paths.

European Commission,
"EU Focus on Clean Air," 1999.

borgh sees a direct connection between cleaner air and climate change in Europe. But he does add a qualification: He says the aerosol effect is not notable year-round. It is only apparent in spring and summer, when days are long and solar radiation is naturally stronger. "But the temperatures in autumn and winter have also risen faster than expected," said van Oldenborgh. There must be another explanation for that phenomenon, he believes.

The Dutch weather institute recently conducted a study on the issue—but the results have yet to be published, and researchers are currently unwilling to discuss preliminary findings. One can assume that changes in air currents during the cold months play a decisive role. There is an increase in fronts from the West transporting warm air from the Atlantic; and at the same time the cold Siberian High is weakened.

Europe's air is not likely to get much cleaner than it is now—neither in summer nor in winter. "The concentration of aerosol is stabile," said ETH Zurich's Wild. And Philipona of the Swiss weather service, is sure that "this increase in temperature, as we saw in Europe in the 1980s, will not happen again."

But this is by no means an announcement that the danger has passed. Greenhouse gases still represent a threat, and increasing and unchecked emissions will almost certainly warm the earth's atmosphere. The German Meteorological Society (DMG) claims that the median temperature in Europe in 2040 will be 1.7 degrees Celsius higher than the median temperature before the Industrial Revolution. Frequent heat waves, severe storms and other extreme weather are a foregone conclusion.

Hong Kong and Taiwanese Air Pollution Is Exacerbated by Chinese Sandstorms

Staff Writers, Hong Kong, Agence France-Presse

Agence France-Presse is an international news agency based in France. In the following viewpoint, the staff notes that the recent Chinese sandstorms have wrought devastating effects on the financial hubs of Hong Kong and Taiwan. The air pollution resulting from the sandstorms has affected the health of residents of both cities.

As you read, consider the following questions:

1. According to doctors at two Taipei hospitals, the March 2010 sandstorm resulted in what kind of increase in patients complaining of respiratory difficulties and eye allergies?

2. How many micrograms of pollutants per hour were measured in each cubic meter of air in Taiwan during the March sandstorm?

3. What was the API reading at one roadside station in Hong Kong on March 22, 2010?

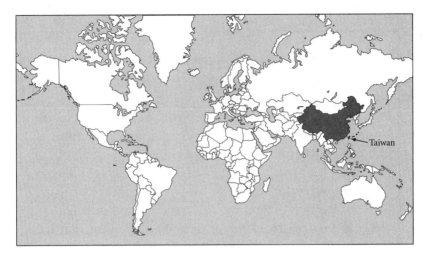

Air pollution in Hong Kong and Taiwan soared to record levels as officials warned Monday [March 22, 2010] of a public health menace from a toxic stew of particulates, fuelled by a massive sandstorm over Beijing.

Readings of Hong Kong's Air Pollution Index [API] were more than double the level at which the general public is advised to stay indoors.

"Today's API is at record high levels," a spokeswoman for the Environmental Protection Department told AFP [Agence France-Presse].

A Public Health Disaster

Hong Kong's famed skyline and harbour is often shrouded in a blanket of haze which has been criticised as a public health disaster and blamed for driving many expatriates away from the international financial hub.

Pollution in nearby Taiwan hit record levels Sunday shrouding the island and forcing authorities on Monday to call on residents to stay indoors.

"This was the first time ever in Taiwan that air pollution was measured to be at such serious levels over such a wide

---

Why Sandstorms Are Prevalent in China

Nature and poor land management practices have combined to create the conditions for a dramatic increase in China's sandstorms over recent years. Sixteen percent of the country's land area is classified as desert, most of it a long-term natural feature of the geography. But to the north and west of Beijing overgrazing, deforestation and urbanisation have all contributed to an adverse weather event that has become an annual occurrence.

Brian Cross,
"The Sandstorms of North China,"
Suite101.com, March 27, 2010.

---

geographic area," said Chang Shun-ching, an official at the Environmental Protection Administration.

"Residents should stay indoors," he said. "For those who need to go out, they had better wear face masks."

Health Effects

Doctors at two Taipei-area hospitals contacted by AFP said the number of outpatients complaining of respiratory difficulties and eye allergies had surged by 30 percent above normal rates.

At all but three monitoring stations in Taiwan, each cubic metre of air was found to contain 1,000 micrograms of pollutants per hour. A level of 150 micrograms per cubic metre per hour is enough for the air quality to be described as "poor".

Chinese authorities warned residents across a huge swathe of the country's north including the capital Beijing to avoid going outside Monday, as the sandstorm blanketed the region in fine yellow dust and a mustard-yellow haze.

Residents complained of coughing and noses clogged with grit, although authorities said the sandstorm was weakening.

Annual Sandstorms in China

Sandstorms are an annual occurrence in arid northern China in the spring when temperatures start to rise, stirring up clouds of dust that can travel across China to South Korea and Japan, and even to the United States.

Scientists blame a combination of deforestation and prolonged drought for the encroachment of desert into more of northern China. The consequences are felt near and wide.

Hong Kong's API is a ratio based on the concentration of pollutants in the air, including sulphur dioxide and lead. Monday's record readings soared as high as 495 at one roadside station.

Sandstorms are an annual occurrence in arid northern China in the spring, when temperatures start to rise, stirring up clouds of dust that can travel across China to South Korea and Japan, and even to the United States.

People with heart or respiratory problems are advised to stay indoors at an API reading of more than 100. The public is advised to stay indoors or avoid prolonged exposure to heavy traffic areas at more than 200.

"This is very scary, over 300 is very scary, very polluted," Edwin Lau, director of Friends of the Earth Hong Kong, told AFP.

Taking No Chances

Schools across Hong Kong kept students indoors, with most cancelling outdoor playground activities and games, or off-campus trips.

"We have stopped any outdoor physical activity or playing to safeguard the children," John Ainsworth, a vice principal at the exclusive Bradbury School, told AFP.

The city's air quality problem was exacerbated by an unusual combination of the Chinese sandstorm and strong southerly winds which blew particulates into the city.

Earlier this month, a group of Hong Kong businesses—including Starbucks, Pacific Coffee, Ben & Jerry's and Pure Fitness—launched an unprecedented petition campaign to combat Hong Kong's worsening air pollution.

The organisers also placed ads in newspapers, warning that the city's smog "kills three people a day" and that its air is "three times dirtier than New York City's".

Periodical and Internet Sources Bibliography

The following articles have been selected to supplement the diverse views presented in this chapter.

Tayo Agunbiade   "Country as a Generator Nation," *This Day* (Nigeria), December 24, 2009.

Eduardo Calvo   "Development Needs to Be Respectful of the Environment," Latinamerica Press, June 24, 2010.

Daily Herald (Zimbabwe)   "Motorists Face Jail over Car Emissions," June 24, 2010.

Daily Trust (Nigeria)   "Growing Trend of Urbanisation, Threat to Health," April 11, 2010.

Alister Doyle   "Russia Fires Cause 'Brown Cloud,' Threaten Arctic," Reuters, August 10, 2010.

Ebenezer Edohasim   "How Lagos Residents Pollute Environment," *Daily Champion* (Nigeria), December 28, 2009.

Andrew Livingstone   "Pollution Puts Brakes on Pedal Power," *China Daily*, July 21, 2010.

Jocelyn Newmarch, Linda Ensor, and Artwell Dlamini   "Environmental Reform—Carbon Tax on New Cars Is Just the Start," *Business Day*, February 18, 2010.

Tom Parfitt   "Smoke from Russian Fires Blankets Moscow," *Guardian* (UK), August 6, 2010.

Nicholas Rainer   "Clearing the Air," lexpress.mu, March 26, 2010.

Mustapha Suleiman   "Acid Rains, the Current Environment Controversy," *Daily Trust* (Nigeria), March 31, 2010.

Times of Zambia   "Lafarge Committed to Clean Environment," June 7, 2010.

Strategies for Reducing Air Pollution

India Uses Giant Air Purifiers to Alleviate Air Pollution

Pratap Chakravarty

Pratap Chakravarty is a writer for Agence France-Presse, an international news agency based in France. In the following viewpoint, the author chronicles India's attempt to improve air quality in New Delhi by using a public air purifier, which is designed to filter out harmful air pollutants such as carbon dioxide and nitrogen oxide. India used the air purifiers in an attempt to clear up the New Delhi smog in anticipation of the Commonwealth Games in late 2010.

As you read, consider the following questions:

1. How much did the air purifier cost?
2. As of March 2010, how many other public purifiers have been installed in other locations?
3. What two Indian cities were ranked among the world's 25 dirtiest cities?

India has switched on its first public air purifier in the heart of capital New Delhi as part of an experiment that backers say could help other smog-choked cities in emerging countries.

Pratap Chakravarty, "India's Smoggy Capital Tries a Whiff of Fresh Air," Agence France-Presse, March 11, 2010. Copyright © 2010 by AGENCE FRANCE-PRESSE. Reproduced by permission.

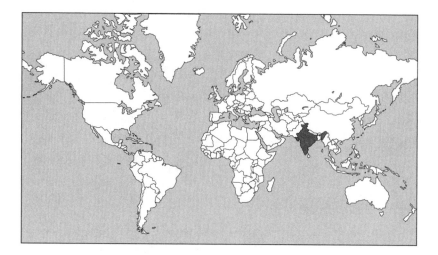

The maker of the seven-ton machine, Italy's Systemlife, claims the box-like structure can purify 10,000 cubic metres of air every hour, scrubbing out pollutants such as carbon dioxide and nitrogen oxide.

A Sign of Things to Come

The unit, plugged in Saturday [March 6, 2010] on a traffic-clogged street of central Delhi, is a pilot that could lead to more being installed in other areas of the city, ranked the world's fourth most polluted by the World Health Organization.

"It is the first such project in India and if it works then we would acquire a number of them and place them at strategic locations," the health chief of the New Delhi Municipal Council, P.K. Sharma, told AFP [Agence France-Presse].

He said a state environmental agency will monitor the performance of the machine, which costs about 25 million rupees (551,000 dollars) and works like a vacuum cleaner, sucking in air and releasing it [in] purified form from a roof vent.

"Money does not matter when health is in question," Sharma said, adding that the purifier would be tested for three months at the site, which is drawing curious onlookers.

The electricity-driven unit, installed free of cost, uses a five-stage filtering process including electrodes to remove health-threatening solid and gaseous pollutants.

"Almost all Indian cities and especially New Delhi needs them," said Ritika Modi, director of the Indian partner company of Systemlife.

The Italian company has installed similar public purifiers at 26 locations in Spain, six in Switzerland and seven in Italian cities, including in the capital Rome, according to a statement issued by the firm.

Assessment of Performance

Environmentalists said they could only give a thumbs-up to the machine after the tests were over, which will include an examination of the filters by the Italian firm after three weeks of operations.

"We have to examine the variation in air quality, but this can be done only after we analyse the readouts," said Vivek Chattopadhyaya, an air analyst with the Centre for Science and Environment, an environmental research and lobby group.

Environmental scientist D. Saha from the Central Pollution Control Board said the state-run watchdog would also keep a check on the success or failure of the Italian unit.

Environmentalists said they could only give a thumbs-up to the machine after the tests were over, which will include an examination of the filters by the Italian firm after three weeks of operations.

In November, the city government vowed to enforce a single standard for industrial and residential pollution as part of plans to tighten air quality rules.

Previous rules allowed lower air quality in industrial areas compared with residential areas.

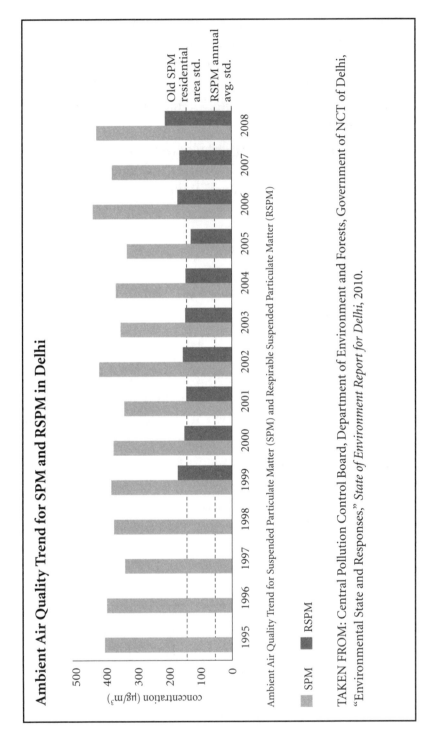

Ambient Air Quality Trend for SPM and RSPM in Delhi

Ambient Air Quality Trend for Suspended Particulate Matter (SPM) and Respirable Suspended Particulate Matter (RSPM)

SPM ■ RSPM

TAKEN FROM: Central Pollution Control Board, Department of Environment and Forests, Government of NCT of Delhi, "Environmental State and Responses," *State of Environment Report for Delhi*, 2010.

Other Air Quality Measures

The city government is also mulling the idea of shutting down thousands of industrial units as well as open-air eateries ahead of the Commonwealth Games later this year in a bid to clear up the city smog.

The Commonwealth Games of October 3–14 [2010] are set to draw 8,000 athletes and officials to New Delhi as well as 100,000 visitors.

In 2008, New Delhi and Indian financial centre Mumbai were ranked among the world's 25 dirtiest cities by *Forbes* magazine.

Global Scientists Propose Biochar as a Cleaner Energy Source

Chris Goodall

Chris Goodall is an author concerned with environmental issues. In the following viewpoint, Goodall considers biochar as a viable solution to deforestation, the global food crisis, and carbon dioxide emissions. In particular, he contends that biochar stoves are much more efficient than traditional wood stoves and have less harmful health effects.

As you read, consider the following questions:

1. According to Professor Johannes Lehmann, how many tonnes of carbon each year could biochar production capture in tropical agricultural systems?
2. What are the advantages of biochar stoves compared to traditional cookstoves?
3. According to one study, how much carbon does a hectare of *terra preta* typically hold compared to adjacent soils?

Hans-Peter Schmidt runs a small organic vineyard in the Swiss Alps. Careful to use no pesticides or artificial fertilisers, he relies on simple techniques to protect against pests and diseases, such as encouraging a wide variety of plants. But Schmidt also does something quite unique among Swiss winemakers to maintain soil fertility. He adds a rich substance known as 'biochar'.

Rediscovering Biochar

A ground-up form of almost pure charcoal, Schmidt's biochar is made from the leftover pips and pulp from his grapes, which he has heated intensely in a kiln. The technique itself is not new: pre-Columbian populations were burning waste to create *terra preta* (black soil) hundreds of years ago, and many people still rely on charcoal-making as a source of cooking fuel. What is new is the sudden interest in biochar as an extraordinarily potent weapon in the fight against climate change. Scientists found that *terra preta* not only created pockets of land in the Amazon which are still extremely fertile 500 years later—but that it kept at least half the carbon in the charcoal 'locked up' for all that time.

Today, many climatologists are as excited as agronomists about biochar. Professor Tim Lenton, from the UK's [United Kingdom's] Tyndall Centre for Climate Change Research, believes that, of all the large-scale solutions under discussion, biochar and reforestation stand out as the most viable options. Professor Johannes Lehmann, an eminent soil specialist from Cornell University, goes so far as to suggest that it is theoretically possible, by the end of this century, that we could capture 9.5 billion tonnes of carbon each year through biochar production in tropical agricultural systems. If we achieved that level of reduction, atmospheric concentrations of carbon dioxide would actually be *falling*. It's no wonder that, in January [2009], Gaia hypothesist James Lovelock told *New Scientist* that "There is one way we could save ourselves, and that is through the massive burial of charcoal".

That prospect came one step closer at last year's Poznan [Poland] climate change conference, where politicians raised the idea of carbon funding for the technique—and there's no doubt the issue will crop up again at Copenhagen this December. If biochar became part of the carbon market, by joining the list of technologies qualifying for the UN's Clean Development Mechanism, we could one day see the rich world offsetting some of its emissions by paying poor farmers to sequester carbon in their soils.

Today, many climatologists are as excited as agronomists about biochar.

Changing Traditional Habits

An example of how this might work is found in Cameroon [in west Africa], where the NGO [nongovernmental organisation] Biochar Fund is giving subsistence farmers, many of them using destructive 'slash and burn' methods of agriculture, the skills to make their own biochar. Run by a young Belgian pioneer, the organisation is working with 75 grassroots groups to produce biochar from materials like palm fronds, cassava stems, weeds and wood, and to test the effects in different soil types. It is developing highly efficient, village-scale kilns which use pyrolysis [a chemical change through heat] to produce both biochar, and heat and electricity ('combined heat, power and char', or CHPC). They could potentially generate money as well by selling carbon credits through the voluntary offset market.

In effect, the Fund is helping farmers shift from 'slash and burn' to 'slash and char' agriculture, by encouraging them not to burn the trees that have been felled but rather to use the wood to make biochar. The char is then added to the soil. It helps improve fertility, enabling the soil to be used for many years, providing more food than can be provided by conventional 'slash and burn', and so reducing the frequency with which new areas of forest need to be cut. For the farmers, this means the chance to develop a more sustainable and prosperous agriculture. For the forests, it means the chance to recover from an increasingly destructive practice. About 400 million people in the Tropics rely on 'slash and burn' agriculture. The benefits for the planet could be huge if they adopted this 'slash and char' method instead.

Biochar Fund's simple ceramic biochar stoves can even be used for cooking while the char is being made, so killing two birds with one stone, as it were. The idea's being taken up in central Asia, too, where the Mongolian Biochar Initiative is supplying simple biochar/cooking stoves to herders, vegetable gardeners and forestry workers. Compared to traditional cookstoves, these use far less fuel for the same amount of cooking. This both reduces the need to cut down more wood and also improves air quality. A large fraction of the world's people do their cooking over open stoves that pollute indoor air, causing respiratory problems and reducing life expectancy.

A large fraction of the world's people do their cooking over open stoves that pollute indoor air, causing respiratory problems and reducing life expectancy.

A Biochar Movement

If they prove viable, such stoves could be sold to poor farmers on a large scale using microcredit to make them affordable—in much the same way that Grameen Shakti, for example, is rolling out improved cooking stoves and solar home systems to villagers in Bangladesh.

This raises the prospect of a mass biochar movement across the developing world. It sounds ambitious, but it would be simple enough to tap into local charcoal-making expertise. The equipment is available locally and soil carbon levels could be measured reasonably accurately with simple devices. A carbon credit system could reward village-level enterprises for producing something to plough back into the soil, rather than something to sell as a fuel.

Stephen Joseph, from Australia's University of New South Wales, has done a cost-benefit analysis of a typical village-scale biochar setup, and found that it could be worth more than $50,000 over five years. This calculation factors in increased yields, savings from planting fewer trees for fuel, reduced medical expenses thanks to less indoor air pollution from smoky stoves—and, of course, carbon credits.

It all sounds too good to be true—and perhaps it is. As biochar has risen up the agenda, it's also attracted its share of sceptics.

Criticism of Biochar

Some argue that, if biochar does indeed become profitable, it could drive deforestation. Writing in the *Guardian*, George Monbiot [an environmental activist] envisages a 'rush' for biochar as we have seen with biofuels. He argues that financial incentives would encourage people to cultivate vast plantations of fast-growing trees in place of ancient forests, or on valuable land needed for food.

Biochar enthusiasts respond that the flow of carbon credits would encourage farmers to continuously harvest and replant trees, using the charcoal to enrich the land as they do so. Chris Turney, professor of geography at the University of Exeter, adds that this type of cyclical scheme would be much more effective at removing emissions from the atmosphere than one-off reforestation schemes, "because mature trees reach a saturation point in their absorption capacity". Meanwhile crop waste—such as straw, husks and leaves—is also a ready source of raw material for biochar. Almost half the nine billion tonnes of agricultural material produced each year is effectively waste material—which contributes to global warming as it rots or is burned off.

More fundamentally, there's the question: does biochar actually work as a carbon sink? Certainly, Amazonian earth would suggest so. One study shows that a hectare of *terra preta* typically holds two and half times the carbon of adjacent soils. Scientists believe biochar can sequester carbon in the soil for hundreds to thousands of years, but they haven't yet calculated its half-life. "We don't have a predictive theory for its behaviour," says Mike Mason, founder of carbon offsetting company Climate Care and bio-energy company Biojoule. "We still need to find out what plant materials should be used, the right temperature for the kiln, what else should be added to the ground. . . ."

Biochar Challenges

There are question marks, too, over whether biochar is universally effective as a soil fertiliser. There are even cases where adding char has been shown to deplete fertility. Current evidence suggests that fertility enhancements seem to be greatest in the Tropics, where soils are often low in other sources of carbon.

Exploratory projects such as those under way in Cameroon and Mongolia should start to provide answers to some of these questions. Along with seven others, they're being closely followed by the International Biochar Initiative—a network of academics, NGOs, investment bankers and politicians looking to promote commercial biochar production.

Developing viable biochar businesses will mean coming up with a business model that rewards everyone involved.

Biochar does not, of course, need to be added to the soil to capture carbon. It can even be buried in underground chambers. This has some superficial similarities with the grand-scale carbon capture and storage (CCS) schemes mooted for coal-fired power stations. But, unlike most CCS schemes, the technology is cheap and simple to install. And, while CCS can only prevent emissions entering the air (at a power station, for example), biochar can 'claw back' carbon that is already out there and seal it in the ground—thanks to its unique way of 'interrupting' a plant's carbon cycle.

Developing viable biochar businesses will mean coming up with a business model that rewards everyone involved. And here, says Mason, "the devil is in the detail". He reminds us that we don't yet have a system that makes economic sense of the complex relationships in biochar production. Who gets the credit?—he asks. "Is it the farmer, because he isn't using so many pesticides? ... If electricity is produced as well, how is this credited?" While there is still this lack of clarity, it may hold back investors from getting involved on a large scale, he says.

Getting Governments Interested

Despite remaining uncertainties, governments are starting to show an interest. The New Zealand Government has included biochar in a $10 million energy research fund; in Australia, the opposition Liberal Party is claiming the technique could cut the country's emissions by a fifth; and the California Energy Commission is hopeful that biochar could be a recognized technology under a proposed new federal cap-and-trade programme. Britain, in comparison, seems a little slow on the uptake. The UK Biochar Research Centre opened late last year at the University of Edinburgh, but the government, for the most part, remains agnostic.

Overall, though, as scientific attention has focused on the benefits of biochar, excitement has grown rather than diminished. As well as its numerous other benefits, biochar stands a good prospect of being one of the simplest, cheapest and most effective ways of capturing carbon dioxide from the atmosphere and storing it safely. One of the world's best-respected earth scientists, Tim Flannery, has described biochar as "the most potent engine of atmospheric cleansing we possess". In a world where the climate news is usually bad, that is one of the few glimmers of real hope.

Scotland Is in Danger of Becoming a Haven for Polluters

Jenny Fyall

Jenny Fyall is a reporter for the Scotsman, *Scotland's daily newspaper. In the following viewpoint, she reports that environmentalists are concerned that Scotland's fines for polluters are so low compared to those in England and Wales that they will do little to deter companies from releasing pollutants into the air. Some government officials and environmentalists are calling for a revised fee system that will act as a true deterrent to polluters.*

As you read, consider the following questions:

1. How much have Scotland's polluter fines dropped since 2006–7?

2. According to the viewpoint, what was the average fine during 2008–9?

3. What was the largest fine handed out by Scotland in 2009–10?

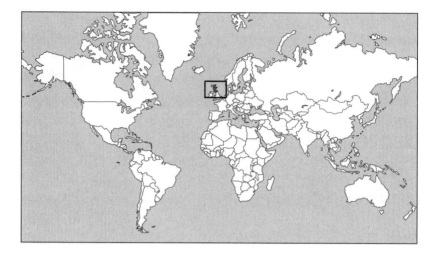

Scotland is at risk of becoming a "polluter haven" due to "derisory" fines doled out for environmental crimes that are almost three times lower than south of the border, experts have warned.

Companies that pollute the environment or illegally dump waste in Scotland are fined on average just over £2,500, in contrast to £7,193 in England and Wales, the *Scotsman* can reveal.

And the fines handed out have dropped dramatically over the past three years, to just over a third of their level in 2006–7, when they averaged £6,500.

Scotland's head of environmental protection said the fines were "derisory" and warned that companies were being actively encouraged to act illegally, because it made good business sense.

In one case, a company saved £100,000 by dumping waste illegally—and was fined just £8,000.

The maximum penalty for the most serious environmental crimes—those decided by a jury—is an unlimited fine or a two-year prison sentence.

However, Scotland's first Enforcement Report for environmental crimes shows the average fine during the financial year 2008–9 was only £2,511.

Debating the Fines

Friends of the Earth Scotland warned the country was at risk of becoming a "polluter haven" unless the legal system for environmental crime was overhauled.

And Colin Bayes, the director of environmental protection at the Scottish Environment Protection Agency (Sepa), which is responsible for policing environmental crimes, said the fines were "unequivocally too low".

Sepa, like the Environment Agency in England and Wales, has powers to recommend that a case be brought to court.

Friends of the Earth Scotland warned the country was at risk of becoming a "polluter haven" unless the legal system for environmental crimes was overhauled.

However, Mr Bayes warned that the sentences resulting from cases heard in Scotland were too low to act as a deterrent.

He called for sentencing guidelines to be drawn up for sheriffs to address the inadequate penalties currently being handed out.

He also argued there was a case for only specialist procurators fiscal to present environmental cases to the courts.

"There is no doubt in my mind that some of the penalties that are issued for environmental criminal offences in Scotland are totally inadequate", Mr Bayes told the *Scotsman*.

"Scotland has got a far better environment on the whole than many parts of England and Wales, so why does our criminal system not appear to value it the same when it has been damaged?"

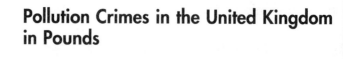

Pollution Crimes in the United Kingdom in Pounds

- Average fine in England and Wales during 2008–9 £7,193

- Average fine in Scotland during 2008–9 £2,511

- Average fine in Scotland during 2006–7 £6,538

- Number of cases referred by Sepa [Scottish Environment Protection Agency] for prosecution during 2008–9 54

- Number of convictions during 2008–9 38 (81%)

- Percentage of fines during 2008–9 that were less than £1,000 38%

Jenny Fyall,
"Scotland Risks Being UK's Pollution 'Haven,'"
Scotsman, February 20, 2010.

Little Punishment for Violators

In one case involving illegal waste, currently subject to an appeal on the grounds of leniency of sentence, a fine of just £8,000 was handed out by the courts for a crime that cost Sepa about £100,000 of taxpayers' money to investigate, and that benefited the culprit by more than £100,000.

More than a third of crimes prosecuted over the past year [2010] have resulted in fines of less than £1,000. The largest penalty was £12,000.

Mr Bayes warned that in some cases it could make good business sense for companies to act illegally. "Without doubt, a lack of deterrent is a big issue, and if a company has carried out an illegal activity knowingly to make money and then gets a derisory fine, it almost encourages such criminal behaviour," he said.

"If you are a company that could make tens of thousands of pounds by dumping materials illegally, and were then fined just £1,000, it would be good business practice to act illegally.

"The fines need to be sufficient to be a deterrent, and clearly the fine levels we have got are, for many offences, inadequate."

A Overhaul of Fee System Is Needed

Duncan McLaren, the chief executive of Friends of the Earth Scotland, said the low fines were "extremely worrying" and added his voice to the call for an overhaul of the legal system for environmental crimes in Scotland.

"The implications are very severe," he said. "If Sepa cannot expect to get deterrent fines levied by the courts, then they can only rely on the carrot, rather than the stick, to try to persuade polluters to improve their performance."

"We will be calling for legislation in the next parliament to improve the situation, so we don't become a polluter haven."

A Holyrood spokeswoman said: "The Scottish Government would encourage Sepa to continue engaging with the Crown Office and the Procurator Fiscal Service, and with other agencies in the justice system, to ensure that fine levels in environmental cases reflect the seriousness of the offence."

However, she added: "Decisions on individual cases, including any penalties to be applied, are entirely a matter for the courts."

South Africa Is Finding a Solution to Burning Tire Pollution

Vuyo Mabandla and Taylor Ervin

Vuyo Mabandla and Taylor Ervin are reporters for Cape Argus, *a Cape Town, South Africa, newspaper. In the following viewpoint, the authors find that the practice of burning tires in some parts of Cape Town, South Africa, has caused major health problems for residents in the region. Government officials are considering legislation to address the issue.*

As you read, consider the following questions:

1. Why do scrap sellers burn tires?
2. What measure is private industry in the region considering to alleviate the problem?
3. What measure is the Cape Town government considering to alleviate the problem?

The city's fire department is at its wits' end with scrap collectors on the Cape Flats who regularly burn tyres and other materials to get at the scrap metal they can sell.

It claims the practice is a major cause of pollution, and constitutes a health risk.

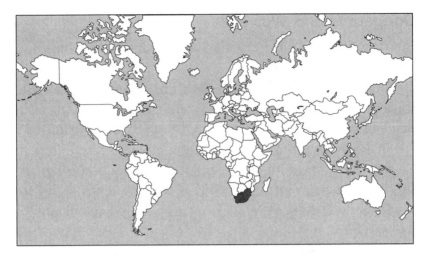

The Practice and Problem

Firefighters at Gugulethu's fire station said people scavenging for scrap metal in the Philippi industrial area burnt tyres continuously, selling the scrap metal to scrap yards just metres away.

During the burning, huge clouds of smoke cover the entire area, spreading to Lower Crossroads and the Luzuko township. Firefighters complained that they were called out repeatedly to the same spot to put out fires.

"We make about five to 10 trips to that place a day—it's tiring. This has been going on for more than three weeks and we are sick and tired of having to come here while there are real emergencies to attend to elsewhere," said one firefighter, who did not wish to be named.

But scrap sellers spoke frankly of how they would never stop, because the practice was their only means of survival. One, Abdullah Samuels of Mitchells Plain, said: "I worry about the environment but I've six kids and a wife to support. I've been doing this for 20 years and I don't see why I should stop now. I am very poor."

Dangerous and Wasteful

But the city has warned that the burning of tyres is dangerous and a waste of resources.

Ian Schnetler, head of the city's fire department, said he was not personally aware of the tyre burnings, but confirmed that similar problems often occurred in parts of Cape Town.

"It is rumoured that a regular response has been registered (in that area), and with all the unnecessary fires occurring, resources are being wasted," he said.

Schnetler was, however, hesitant to put an actual figure to the wastage.

In the area in question, thick bush has been replaced by the remains of chemical waste, burnt animal carcasses and building materials.

Consequences of Burning Tyres

Residents said they worried about their health, while initiates settled on the land complained that the toxic smoke made it difficult for them to heal.

Mother-of-four Belinda Plaatjie, 26, whose six-month-old daughter has respiratory problems, said the thick smoke would cover her entire house.

"I've developed eye problems. They're always itching and watering and I have no doubt it's the fires. I'm scared that my children might develop some sicknesses as well," she said.

Residents said they worried about their health, while initiates settled on the land complained that the toxic smoke made it difficult for them to heal.

Dumisani Zingisile, an initiate, said: "This is a dire health risk. Something should be done about it."

Ivan Bromfield, head of health in the city, agreed the burning of tyres posed a major health risk: "The acrid smoke is a nuisance and can be a health problem to those living in close proximity to where the burning takes place. Open burning of wastes generates excessive emissions of pollutants such as dense and odorous smoke, dust and toxic fumes," he said.

Measures to Address Issue

Schnetler urged scrap dealers to consider the environment when buying scrap, but branch manager at the SA Metal Group, Lindsay Naidoo, said they were aware of the problem. "We have banned people with scrap metal obtained from burnt objects," he said.

Bromfield said the city was amending the current Air Pollution Control bylaw to make provision for officials to prosecute anyone found in possession of, transporting or storing burnt scrap metal, including tyres. The new bylaw would come into effect in July [2010].

Israel Passes a Clean Air Law

Adam Teva V'Din - Israel Union for Environmental Defense

The Israel Union for Environmental Defense (IUED) is Israel's leading environmental advocacy organization. In the following viewpoint, the group celebrates the 2008 Clean Air Law that passed in Israel and expects it will usher in a new era in environmental governance in the country. The law centralizes responsibility for air quality management under the Ministry of Environmental Protection.

As you read, consider the following questions:

1. What American resources did the IUED turn to for help in crafting a clean air bill?

2. What nongovernmental organization (NGO) did IUED work with to raise public awareness of the need for a clean air law?

3. How will IUED continue to be involved in the effort to improve air quality in Israel?

"The Clean Air Law (2008) is the most complex and innovative environmental law passed in Israel," states Tzipi Iser Itzik, IUED [Israel Union for Environmental Defense] executive director and one of the team of attorneys and scientists working on the law at IUED from the bill's inception seven years ago. "We are on the threshold of a new era in

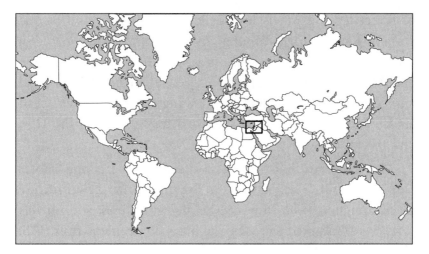

environmental governance in Israel," adds Iser Itzik. "The law promises a healthier future for us all."

After years of intensive preparation and a rocky five-year journey through the Knesset [the Israeli legislature], the Clean Air bill was approved on July 22, 2008. Israel now joins the ranks of developed countries using comprehensive legislative tools to plan, regulate and monitor air quality.

The law provides a systematic arrangement of authority in relation to air quality management (industry, transport, electricity, fuel, monitoring and enforcement authorities) that were until now scattered among government agencies. The onus of responsibility for air quality management will now be shouldered by the Ministry of Environmental Protection.

> *Israel now joins the ranks of developed countries using comprehensive legislative tools to plan, regulate and monitor air quality.*

Why Not a Clean Air Law for Israel, Too?

During its first decade of environmental advocacy, IUED's efforts to reduce air pollution were often stymied by the dearth of direct legal channels for challenging polluters and by the scattering of authority among government agencies operating under different guidelines and priorities. In 2001, IUED's then executive director, Philip Warburg, challenged IUED's legal and scientific staff to begin formulating a proposal for a clean air law along the lines of established frameworks in the USA and the European Union.

"We soon realized this was a massive undertaking," notes Tzipi Iser Itzik. "Contacts at the Environmental Law Institute in Washington, D.C., provided helpful guidelines, and our efforts were bolstered by advice and encouragement from U.S. Congressman Henry Waxman, one of the 'fathers' of the American clean air law."

From Private Bill to Knesset Vote

By 2003, the draft was ready for adoption as a parliamentary bill. "We asked then Knesset member Omri Sharon, at the time joint leader with Rabbi Michael Melchior, of the Knesset's cross-party environmental caucus," relates Dvora Sylas Fruman, IUED's Knesset liaison. Sharon reviewed the bill's thirty-page draft and consulted with colleagues and advisors before agreeing to put it forward as a private member's bill. "He quickly showed his commitment by getting other MKs [members of Knesset] on board."

There followed many months of intensive meetings and negotiations with the professional staff of the Environment Ministry, the Treasury and nine other government agencies. "At this point, it was crucial to get important stakeholders like the Manufacturers Association, representing most of Israel's industrial plants, and the Israel Electric Corporation, to sit with us and thrash out pivotal components of the bill," recalls Tzipi Iser Itzik. "We worked productively with agencies that hitherto had been on the other side of the barricades in IUED's battles for clean air," recounts Iser Itzik.

By the end of December 2005, the bill passed its preliminary reading before the 16th Knesset, securing its place on the legislative agenda and guaranteeing it continuity of review before the 17th Knesset.

Those in Charge

Knesset member Rabbi Moshe Gafni then became the bill's main sponsor, supported by the environmental caucus. Dr. Dov Khenin headed the special subcommittee handling the bill under the auspices of the Knesset's standing committee on Interior & Environment. As the stakeholders reached agreement on the substance of the bill—by then expanded way beyond its original 30 pages—the chair of the Interior & Environment committee, MK Ophir Pines-Paz, took responsibility for getting the bill to its second and third readings. IUED's clean air team remained an active partner in the review and redraft process, to a degree unprecedented for an NGO [nongovernmental organization].

"Our professional know-how and determination not to let the bill get sidetracked and watered down were vital," points out Iser Itzik. "We took every opportunity to bring home to Knesset members, government agencies, and industry stakeholders that the bill had the potential to reduce the number of Israelis suffering disease and death every year as a result of air pollution."

Coalition for Clean Air

In parallel, IUED worked with its environmental NGO partners . . . to raise public awareness of the importance of the law through campaigning and petition-signing. "While we were banging on tables demanding that transparency and public participation be integrated into certain clauses of the bill, our friends from Green Course were working the streets getting people to sign petitions and letters to decision makers," recalls Iser Itzik. "Demonstrations outside the Knesset helped bring the message that we weren't going to give up."

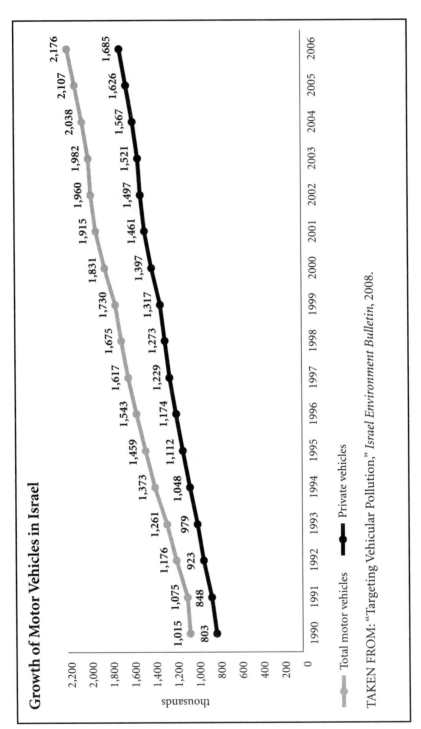

Growth of Motor Vehicles in Israel

thousands

Total motor vehicles

Private vehicles

TAKEN FROM: "Targeting Vehicular Pollution," *Israel Environment Bulletin*, 2008.

Change in the Air

There were many stops and starts along the way, especially when the Treasury raised objections because of potentially high costs to the economy. By May 2008, the bill was ready to go before the Knesset plenary for its second and third readings. At this point, the Environment Ministry wavered, and Minister Gideon Ezra asked for additional review and budgetary allocations to enable his ministry to take on additional staff and to reorganize in preparation for administering and enforcing the law.

MK Pines-Paz determinedly pushed ahead and by July, the Clean Air bill was presented to the Knesset, albeit with a number of 'reservations' proffered by government ministries. These were integrated into the final proposal, and at long last, the bill was approved by the Knesset on July 22, 2008.

The Clean Air Law (2008) is a triumph for the environmental movement and a victory for every Israeli subject to polluted air from factories, transport and power stations.

"If You Will It, It Is No Legend"

The Clean Air Law (2008) is a triumph for the environmental movement and a victory for every Israeli subject to polluted air from factories, transport and power stations.

"We are very proud that our dream of a modern and stringent clean air law is coming into being," says Tzipi Iser Itzik. "None of us can rest on our laurels, however. The Environment Ministry has two short years in which to be ready with a national strategy for air quality." In addition, there are dozens of regulations, emissions standards, compliance procedures, penalties and other tools for implementing the law to be decided upon. Close monitoring and participation by IUED will be part of the implementation stage.

"IUED will continue to be closely involved," notes IUED's director. She vows that IUED will devote similar energy and determination to making the law workable and enforceable and that IUED will work to make sure that the public has a real say in how the government tackles the challenge of improving air quality. "Now Israel has a clean air law, there are no more excuses for inaction on reducing health threatening air pollution."

Canada Pioneers the Use of Carbon Capture and Storage Systems

Stephen Harper

Stephen Harper is the Prime Minister of Canada. In the following viewpoint excerpted from a speech, he praises the state-of-the-art carbon capture and storage system installed in the Keephills power plant in Alberta, contending that it will reduce carbon emissions from the plant by an estimated million tonnes a year. Harper asserts that the technology will secure Canada's position as a world leader in the implementation of green technology.

As you read, consider the following questions:

1. According to the Carbon Capture and Storage Task Force, carbon capture and storage could eliminate what percentage of Canada's greenhouse gas emissions by 2050?

2. What is it about the storage system at the Keephills plant that makes it the first of its kind in the world?

3. What does Harper believe is the key to encouraging the use of carbon capture and storage around the world?

Stephen Harper, "Clean Energy for Tomorrow: Investing in Carbon Capture and Storage in Alberta," Office of the Prime Minister of Canada, Prime Minister Stephen Harper, October 14, 2009. http://pm.gc.ca/eng/media.asp?id=2888. Reproduced with the permission of the Minister of Public Works and Government Services, 2010, and Courtesy of the Privy Council Office.

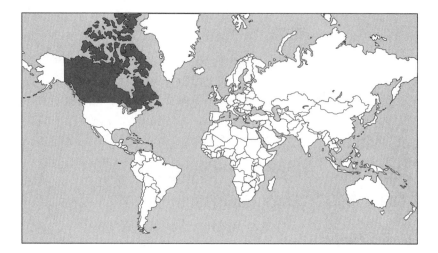

During the worst global recession in half a century, our government's number one priority has been, and continues to be, protecting the Canadian economy. Our Economic Action Plan is creating jobs. It is stimulating our economy. And it is supporting Canadians hardest hit by the recession.

Looking to the Future

But, at the same time, our plan is focused on the long term, focused on positioning Canada for unprecedented future success. To keep Canada on the cutting edge we are investing massively in scientific and technological research and development. And a major focus of these investments is our energy sector.

As I have told audiences around the world, Canada is an emerging energy superpower. But, as you all well know, the only way we are going to stay competitive in the global energy market of the future, is if we are also a clean energy superpower. We must develop new, clean sources of energy, and we must develop technologies that make cleaner use of conventional energy. And that's what brings us together for today's important announcement.

Carbon capture and storage has the potential to help us balance our need for energy, with our duty to protect the environment. In fact, according to the Carbon Capture and Storage Task Force, the technology could eliminate almost one half of Canada's greenhouse gas emissions by 2050. That's why our Economic Action Plan includes a one billion dollar Clean Energy Fund, most of which is being devoted to large-scale carbon capture and storage demonstration projects.

Carbon capture and storage could not only drastically reduce our emissions, but by exporting it to other countries, we could also make a major contribution to the reduction of global emissions.

Only One of Its Kind

Today, I am pleased to announce that we are partnering with the Government of Alberta and TransAlta [Corp.] to retrofit the Keephills power plant with a fully integrated carbon capture and storage system; the only one of its kind in Canada, ladies and gentlemen!

The aptly named "Pioneer Project" will reduce carbon emissions from the plant by a million tonnes a year. And with a completely integrated underground storage system, this plant will not just be a first for Canada; indeed, it will be the first of its kind in the world!

I want to thank Premier [Ed] Stelmach and his government, for joining us in this bold venture. And I want to thank TransAlta for taking a leadership role in developing this critical technology. Innovations like carbon capture and storage will define the future of this industry.

I'd also like to take a moment to acknowledge the workers here at the Keephills plant who will make this project a reality. Like the 19th-century coal miners and the 20th-century wildcatters who gave birth to the Alberta energy industry, history

What Is Carbon Capture and Storage (CCS)?

Carbon is emitted into the atmosphere (as carbon dioxide, also called CO_2) whenever we burn any fossil fuel, anywhere. The largest sources are cars and lorries [trucks], and power stations that burn fossil fuels: coal, oil or gas. To prevent the carbon dioxide building up in the atmosphere (probably causing global warming and definitely causing ocean acidification), we can catch the CO_2, and store it. As we would need to store thousands of millions of tons of CO_2, we cannot just build containers, but must use natural storage facilities. Some of the best natural containers are old oil and gas fields, such as those in the North Sea.

UK Carbon Capture and Storage Community,
"What Is Carbon Capture and Storage?" 2009.
www.co2storage.org.uk.

will remember you as the pioneers who transformed the industry in the 21st century, as the pioneers who kept Alberta at the forefront of the global energy market, as the pioneers who contributed to a prosperous future for all of Canada!

Carbon Capture and Storage Is the Future

Ladies and gentlemen, our government is determined that Canada remains a world leader in the use of this state-of-the-art technology. Carbon capture and storage could not only drastically reduce our emissions, but by exporting it to other countries, we could also make a major contribution to the reduction of global emissions. Raising awareness about this technology is key to encouraging its use around the world. That's why, as I announced last summer [July 2009] at the G-8 [Group of 8, an annual economic, trade, and political forum for eight of the world's leading industrialized nations] in Italy, Canada helped found the Global Carbon Capture and Storage Institute. And why our government worked with the International Energy Agency to establish a CO_2 monitoring and storage program in Saskatchewan. What's more, as host of the G-8 and G-20 [Group of 20, a forum for the finance ministers and central bank governors of 19 industrialized and developing countries plus the European Union to discuss international economic issues] summits next year [2010], Canada will have another opportunity to showcase our leadership in carbon capture and storage to the world.

We are taking real action at home and on the world stage to produce real, tangible reductions in greenhouse gas emissions. As a government, we are committed to a cleaner, healthier environment for all Canadians, and for generations to come. By investing in projects like this one, our Economic Action Plan is helping achieve these important goals.

Staying on Course

As I have said, now is not the time for political uncertainty or instability. Now is the time to stay on course, to finish implementing our plan, and to strengthen the foundations of Canada's future prosperity!

By looking forward today, and supporting projects like the one here at Keephills, we are seizing the opportunities that will get us through these difficult times and ensure that our country, Canada, emerges stronger than ever.

London Formulates Clean Air Strategy

Greater London Authority

The Greater London Authority (GLA) is a regional governmental authority formed to help implement the plans of the London Mayor and improve the quality of life in the city. In the following viewpoint, the GLA discusses the air quality improvement proposals in Mayor Boris Johnson's draft (public consultation closed on August 13, 2010) of the "Clearing the Air" strategy. Proposals include improving electric vehicle infrastructure, streamlining traffic flow, eliminating older vans and minibuses, and creating a low emission zone for heavier polluting vehicles.

As you read, consider the following questions:

1. According to a recent House of Commons Environmental Audit Committee report, how many deaths in the United Kingdom per year can be attributed to the effects of air pollution?

2. According to a study commissioned by Boris Johnson, how many people a year in London could be dying prematurely due to the impact of poor air quality?

3. How many charging points for electric vehicles does London plan on having by spring 2013?

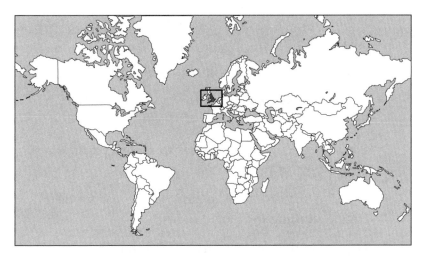

The Mayor of London [Boris Johnson] has set out detailed plans to tackle air pollution hot spots to ensure London meets legal targets for particulate matter by 2011 and that 250km [kilometres] of the dirtiest roads meet NO_2 [nitrogen dioxide] legal targets by 2015.

Mayor's Plan Is Now Public

'Clearing the Air', the Mayor's air quality strategy, is now out for public consultation, with a range of pollution-busting measures to reduce concentrations of particulate matter (PM_{10}) by an estimated 10 to 20 per cent at priority areas in central London. These include: Marylebone Road, Euston Road, Marble Arch, Hyde Park Corner, Victoria Embankment, Upper Thames Street and Tower Hill.

The latest figures show London is on track to meet PM_{10} legal limits by 2011, but these areas have been identified as being most at risk of breaching limits when weather conditions are poor.

Actions to target these areas will be undertaken in partnership with local boroughs and Transport for London following months of detailed discussion. Potential solutions that could be applied depending on each location include:

- Power washing the roads to remove harmful particulates from traffic;

- Applying dust suppressants on road surfaces;

- Changes to signal timings to smooth the flow of traffic;

- Planting green walls and trees to absorb particulates and to protect pedestrians;

- No-idling enforcement to stop people leaving their engine running for long periods;

- Deploying the cleanest buses along these routes.

In addition, the strategy proposes measures to clean up roads across London so that 250km more of London's roads will meet legal targets for NO_2 by 2015 which would otherwise have breached these limits. This includes retrofitting older buses with equipment to bring them up to cleaner Euro 4 standards for NO_x [nitrogen oxide] and the introduction of a new NO_x standard for larger vehicles that have to comply with the Low Emission Zone standards.

The Mayor has also proposed today [March 28, 2010] that—subject to statutory public consultation on the implementation date—the oldest, most polluting heavier vans and minibuses will be included in the Low Emission Zone from January 2012.

Air quality is an issue that affects all cities and towns across the country.

Green Transportation

In addition, the Mayor has committed to work with the vehicle manufacturing industry to develop an affordable black cab that emits 60 per cent less pollution by 2015, and a zero-emission black cab by 2020. The Mayor has proposed to introduce age limits for taxis and minicabs to ensure the most polluting of these vehicles are removed from London's roads subject to consultation with the taxi and private hire vehicle trade.

The Mayor is also discussing with London Councils how the London Lorry Control Scheme can be used to incentivise a cleaner 'London lorry' standard that will deliver substantial improvements in freight emissions.

This is in addition to over £250m [million] that the GLA [Greater London Authority] is already spending on measures, which are improving the capital's air quality. Air quality is an issue that affects all cities and towns across the country. The recent House of Commons Environmental Audit Committee report estimated that air pollution could be contributing to as many as 50,000 deaths in the UK [United Kingdom] per year. Early results of a study commissioned by the Mayor to be published later this year [2010] suggests that around 4,300 people a year in London could be dying prematurely, mainly as a result of the impact of poor air quality on pre-existing conditions such as asthma, heart disease and respiratory illness.

The Mayor has today joined the Committee in calling on the Government to commit the resources necessary to reduce the enormous burden air pollution places on organisations such as the NHS [National Health Service] and to implement national measures where they are most effective: such as a national framework for certifying vehicle retrofitting and raising public awareness of the challenges faced in tackling air quality, incentives for fleet managers to retrofit their vehicles to make them cleaner, an extended vehicle scrappage scheme targeted at particular vehicle types (e.g., vans, minibuses and taxis) and better-coordinated and funded energy efficiency schemes for homes and workplaces and electrification of London's rail network.

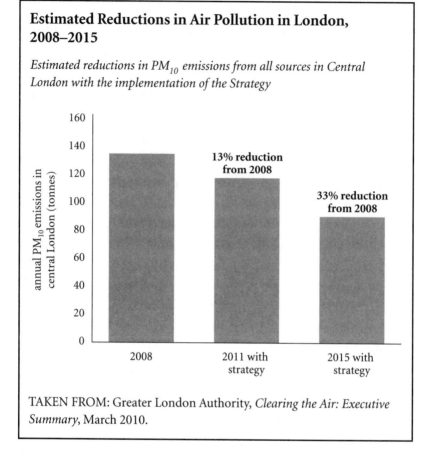

Estimated Reductions in Air Pollution in London, 2008–2015

Estimated reductions in PM$_{10}$ emissions from all sources in Central London with the implementation of the Strategy

annual PM$_{10}$ emissions in central London (tonnes)

13% reduction from 2008

33% reduction from 2008

2008   2011 with strategy   2015 with strategy

TAKEN FROM: Greater London Authority, *Clearing the Air: Executive Summary*, March 2010.

Crafting a Comprehensive Policy

The Mayor Boris Johnson said: 'We are taking tough action to clean up London's air by targeting measures where they will have the most impact. These are creating a city where buses and taxis are becoming progressively less polluting, where cycling and transport choices such as electric vehicles will become more widespread.

'As part of this drive for a cleaner city, from January 2012, I am proposing to push ahead with the inclusion of heavier vans and minibuses in the Low Emission Zone. We are also planning to introduce age limits on taxis to eradicate the oldest, dirtiest vehicles. As part of this work, we are talking to manufacturers to develop a wonderful new black cab that emits no fumes by 2020.

'But London simply cannot crack this pressing problem alone, not least because a significant amount of pollution is blown in from outside our boundaries. It is estimated that air quality is contributing to the deaths of up to 50,000 people every year across the UK. That is why I am calling on the Government to implement and provide adequate funding for initiatives that will tackle pollution in London. We've set out specific measures we're calling on Government to adopt that we believe will enable compliance with all limit values.'

Dame Helena Shovelton, chief executive of the British Lung Foundation said: 'We welcome the Mayor's proposed air quality strategy for London. Any initiative, which reduces harmful emissions for Londoners, is a positive step forward, particularly for the 1 in 7 affected by lung conditions such as chronic obstructive pulmonary disease (COPD) and asthma as it can worsen their symptoms. Improving the air we breathe should mean fewer premature deaths, reduced hospital visits, and fewer GP [general practitioner] consultations for people with respiratory disease.'

These detailed proposals form part of a public draft of the Mayor's air quality action plan, which is now open to consultation. The strategy outlines the key sources of London's harmful airborne pollutants and proposes an action plan to reduce emissions. The pollutants of particular concern are nitrogen dioxide (NO_2) and particulate matter (PM_{10})—road transport is the main source of emissions—with emissions from gas used in homes and businesses also a large contributor of NO_2. A significant proportion of pollution is also blown into London from outside the capital.

Work Has Already Started

The Mayor is already implementing a range of measures in London to improve air quality such as introducing a hybrid

bus fleet, record levels of investment in cycling and programmes to cut domestic and commercial emissions. The
New Bus for London, due to enter service in 2012, will incor-
porate the latest hybrid technology and will be both 40 per
cent more fuel efficient than conventional diesel buses and 15
per cent more fuel efficient than current London hybrid buses.

The Mayor also has ambitious plans to make London the
electric vehicle capital of Europe—this took a major step forward recently with the confirmation of up to £17 million additional funding for electric vehicle infrastructure. This will
deliver a network of around 7,500 charging points by spring
2013 with around 1,600 charge points to be installed over the
next 12 months.

---

*The Mayor [Boris Johnson] is already implementing a
range of measures in London to improve air quality such
as introducing a hybrid bus fleet, record levels of investment in cycling and programmes to cut domestic and
commercial emissions.*

But the Government faces large fines of potentially millions of pounds from the European Union if legal air quality
limits are not met across the UK.

Implementation of the policies and proposals in the strategy is expected to reduce PM_{10} emissions in central London
by around 13 per cent by 2011 and by about a third by 2015
(compared to 2008). Together with the targeted local measures
in priority areas, modelling suggests that this will allow London to be compliant with legal limits by 2011. The strategy
will also see NO_x emissions fall by 35 per cent by 2015
(compared to 2008 levels). However, NO_2 is a national issue
requiring further action from central Government. The Mayor
is calling on the Government to introduce national measures,
which will deliver benefits in London and across the country.

Together with the measures in the Mayor's strategy, these will meet NO_2 limit values in London by 2015.

South Africa Makes Fuel from Rubbish

Emily Miller

Emily Miller is a reporter for African Business. *In the following viewpoint, Miller reports on the new method of converting trash into clean transport fuel, developed by the Centre of Material and Process Synthesis (COMPS) in Johannesburg. According to the developers, the process can use either conventional feedstock such as coal or the unconventional feedstock of rubbish to produce fuel. The process emits 30 percent less carbon dioxide than comparative processes, and the developers have a version that converts carbon dioxide and hydrogen into liquid hydrocarbons. COMPS claims that the process lessens the problem of methane from landfills. Although the energy output of the process cannot compete with nuclear power, the developers claim that it can be competitive on cost.*

As you read, consider the following questions:

1. What process developed in the 1920s is the new process based on, and how long has that original process been in use in South Africa?

2. What does Canada's Alternative Fuels Corporation (AFC) say about the fuel-from-rubbish system?

Emily Miller, "Fuel—How to Have Your Cake and Eat It: With the Kyoto Protocol Pushing for a 30% Cut in Greenhouse Gas Emissions by 2020, Industry Worldwide Urgently Needs a Revolutionary Alternative to 'Dirty' Fuels Like Oil and Coal. Now a Team of South African Engineers Believes It Has Cracked the Problem with an Ingenious Solution. Emily Miller Reports from Cape Town," *African Business*, August–September, 2009. Copyright © 2009 IC Publications Ltd. Reproduced by permission.

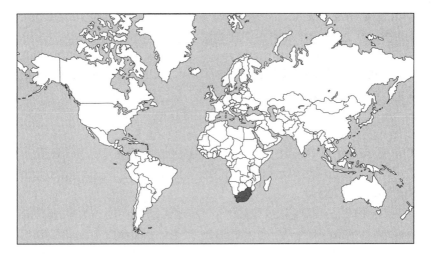

3. How has COMPS improved on the old conversion
   method developed in the 1920s?

The Centre of Material and Process Synthesis (COMPS) in
Johannesburg [South Africa] has developed a new method
of turning industrial levels of everyday rubbish into ultra-
clean transport fuel. The chemical reaction system, which
gives 2.7 barrels of synthetic oil for each tonne of rubbish,
emits 30% less carbon dioxide than comparative processes.

A low-cost scheme, it is being considered as a means of
waste disposal by governments worldwide including in Dubai,
Canada and Morocco. Experts at COMPS, part of the University of the Witwatersrand, realise the concept of turning garbage into power may be a hard sell. To inspire investor confi-
dence, their system has also been designed to process more
conventional feedstocks. In September [2009], work will start
on the first commercial plant in China, running on coal to
produce 3m tonnes of transport fuel a year.

COMPS project manager Dr Brendon Hausberger said:
"Sustainable energy is what we do. Tonne for tonne, you get
the same output whether you put in waste or coal. We're the
first in the world to be putting this into commercial practice,

which shows our ideas are cost effective. Industry bosses are bound to have greater initial faith in conventional feedstocks like coal, but actually they would have an equally productive experience with rubbish. This is not radical mumbo jumbo. It's a very practical solution."

A COMPS facility producing 28,000 barrels a day would earn $250m [million] a year from coal or $230m from waste. The process is based on tried-and-tested Fischer-Tropsch, a catalysed chemical reaction model developed in Germany in the 1920s.

Used by petrol giant Sasol in South Africa for 50 years, the system continues to produce 30% of the country's liquid fuels today, and after 17 years of research, COMPS has now evolved a version that converts carbon dioxide and hydrogen into liquid hydrocarbons, excluding poisonous carbon monoxide used in the original method.

They say it is cleaner, more flexible and carries lower start-up costs. Dr Hausberger explains: "It's basically molecular recycling. Less carbon is lost to the atmosphere—which means more energy contained inside your system to produce fuel."

In June, Canada's Alternative Fuels Corporation (AFC) signed an agreement to promote COMPS as a fuel-from-rubbish system across the Americas. AFC business vice president, Michael Hepworth, told *African Business*: "Waste has the lowest carbon footprint of all fuels. It's inexpensive compared to coal, which admittedly carries 50% more energy but is hugely capital intensive.

"This new system lessens the landfill problem of methane, a greenhouse gas 21 times more harmful than [CO_2]. I'm not sure waste will ever replace fossil fuels, but every city with more than a million people should have a plant of this nature. We're talking to people in Brazil, Argentina, and across the US about deployment within the next few years." AFC has pinpointed a site near Sarnia, Ontario, where the first facility is expected to open.

The merits of nuclear power—principally a vastly increased output rate—are a hot topic at South African energy firm Eskom, whose proposed Pebble Bed Modular Reactor has been delayed by government. Plant for plant, COMPS admits, their production speed will never compete, but dollar for dollar they believe it can. "Per unit of power production in plant, a coal- or waste-fed facility will always be cheaper," says Hausberger, adding "the safety requirements would be less".

COMPS hopes this African technology will be a chance for the continent to take a global lead. Hausberger says: "The developing world has a chance here to learn from the mistakes of more advanced nations. Africans have learned to make the most of what they've got. The idea of putting waste to good use is just an extension of those habits."

For a quota of rubbish produced by 120,000 people, the COMPS system requires a workforce of 350 to produce 900 barrels of fuel per day. A four-tonne batch of commercial waste—such as paper, plastic bottles, foam or shredded rubber—yields six barrels (one tonne) of fuel.

The same ratio will operate with coal at the upcoming COMPS facility in China, which is set to produce 50,000 barrels daily. Depending on oil prices, a payback period of three to five years is expected by the Golden Nest Technology Group, who financed the project. The Baodan Liquid Fuels Plant in Baoji, Shaanxi Province, is the extension of a demonstration model launched in 2007. It has inspired investors in Vietnam and India to look at a rollout plan.

A COMPS pilot site tested by Australian innovators Line Energy in Chinchilla, Queensland, currently produces 15 barrels a day and may be implemented on an industrial scale. Hausberger confirms: "Firms like us because we're radically shifting the goalposts. The old Fischer-Tropsch model gave [CO_2] emissions of 7.5 tonnes per tonne of fuel. We've cut it to 6.5 tonnes. What's more, we've cut the feedstock to output ratio from 5:1 to 4:1."

COMPS, who have consulted for mining magnates De Beers and Anglo Platinum, hope to score points with the corporations' Environmental Impact Assessments through an improved return on energy investment. Instead of requiring oxygen, gleaned by a costly additional procedure, the new process just needs air.

Its 'once-through' system means a third of the molecules—often otherwise wasted within the cycle—make it straight through into the product. The synthetic oil produced is then refined into transport fuels: diesel, gasoline and jet fuel. All are low in sulphur and nitrogen. Unpopular aromatics like benzine, blacklisted in the international drive to create a green fuel mass market, are few. And looking to the future, firms who aim to feed their fuel generator using gases produced by nuclear, wind, or bio systems will find COMPS uses precisely the same ones: carbon dioxide and hydrogen.

Flexible and Cheaper

Yet for the billions worldwide, the demand remains 'cheap energy, fast'. Tapping into this market, COMPS has devised a building-block approach for firms with limited up-front cash—ideal for emerging markets. This has aroused the interest of potential clients in South Africa, Zimbabwe, Congo, Nigeria and Botswana.

If a cluster of municipalities gets off the ground with one COMPS module costing $100m, the outfit can later expand using revenue earned through their biofuel. Hausberger notes: "What we are looking at is a technology where you can put in what's affordable and be up and running. In Africa, the market is wide open for something new. But capital is not abundant and the future is far from certain.

"But our low start-up costs let each plant grow at its own rate. When money starts coming in, modules can be added. For instance, today's Zimbabwe has neither a steady local market nor reliable export demand. But if it manages to start now with what little it has and grow later, it won't have wasted time during the relatively poor years."

COMPS also promotes 'low-risk' machinery—diesel engines produced and serviced in Africa, rather than European gas turbines. Hausberger says: "Our engines are known to African workers, who can fix them without having to waste operational downtime looking abroad for parts or know-how."

Critics argue that turbines produce around 5% less $[CO_2]$—but COMPS counters this advantage by its overall carbon emission saving of 30%. Another major advantage is the creation of jobs—not only for those operating the machines, but also in the low-skilled sector of waste sorting.

Hausberger, who has partnered with UK recycling developer Cierra, confirms: "Picking out materials is a manual task. It needs people." What starts out as a heap of rubbish also becomes a lucrative source of recyclable materials such as aluminium. The reaction itself throws up further by-product commodities including high-quality wax for printing and pharmaceuticals and organic solvents for the chemical industry and electricity.

A 900-barrel-a-day facility on a three to six-month start-up period would use 1,500 tonnes of waste a day to produce 17 megawatts. That's enough to power 18,000 domestic hot-water geysers. By reversing the gas conversion process, the COMPS system could also produce plastics and polymers.

Final-stage talks are under way to see a COMPS municipal plant built in Dubai within two years, capable of accepting 50 tonnes of waste a day. A single module costing $25111 to $30m is planned to be running by 2012, with the option to add 50 more.

Aside from the fuel produced to power public transport, a revenue stream would come from a by-product of wood substitute sold to United Arab Emirates construction firms. Hausberger adds: "You could expect a firm to pay tipping fees of up to $12 a tonne, just to have their waste taken away. The US produces a billion tonnes of waste a year. That quantity could produce a billion tonnes of energy.

"This is Africa's chance to show the world a new way of doing things. If people make the change, they really can have their cake and eat it too!"

Egypt Debates Policies to Eliminate Its "Black Cloud" of Pollution

Hoda Baraka

Hoda Baraka is a Cairo-based environmental consultant and teaching assistant at the American University in Cairo. In the following viewpoint, Baraka argues that government attempts to address the "Black Cloud" of air pollution that hovers over Cairo, the capital of Egypt, every year have failed because of insufficient regulations and a lack of effective enforcement. Baraka asserts that environmental activism may be the main lever of change on this issue.

As you read, consider the following questions:

1. When did the Black Cloud first appear, according to Baraka?
2. How many industrial factories are located in Cairo?
3. According to the viewpoint, what measures has the Egyptian government taken to address the Black Cloud?

I t seems that the Black Cloud phenomenon has become, not only part of our yearly rituals, but of our daily lives [in Cairo, Egypt].

Hoda Baraka, "Egypt's Permanent Black Cloud," *Daily News Egypt / International Herald Tribune*, December 21, 2008. Copyright © 2008 by *Daily News Egypt / International Herald Tribune*. Reproduced by permission.

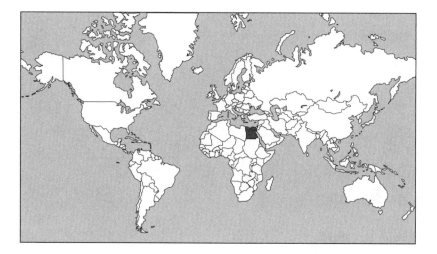

The first time the Black Cloud appeared was in the autumn of 1999 and it's been a recurrent phenomenon ever since. Breaking down the scientific factors causing it would be the first step towards eradicating this annual air pollution climax.

Factors That Cause Black Cloud

One of these factors is a natural phenomenon. It involves a meteorological occurrence called 'thermal inversion' whereby a warm air cap forms over Cairo. This air cap, however, neither rises nor subsides, hence trapping the air pollution instead of allowing it to disperse.

Other factors are man-induced and include: industrial pollution caused by the fact that Cairo houses an estimate of 12,600 factories; transportation—the approximate number of vehicles on the streets of Cairo already surpassed the 2 million mark with an average increase of 10 percent annually.

Also, the burning of rice straw, which takes place every October, aggravates the problem especially when done in conjunction with the open air burning of garbage since there is no solid waste management system in place.

Real Reasons for Black Cloud

"Every day, some two million cars hit the streets of greater Cairo, which is also surrounded by industrial factories and both of these represent bigger pollutants than the straw burning," he [Mohamed Nagi, head of the Hapi Centre for Environmental Rights] said. "While straw burning certainly contributes to a rising carbon content in the air, vehicle emissions are just as much—if not more—to blame."

Adam Morrow and Khaled Moussa Al-Omrani,
"Darkness at Noon Clouds Cairo Skies,"
IPS News, *December 10, 2009. http://ipsnews.net.*

Measures to Curb the Cloud Have Failed

Although the Egyptian government has in recent years introduced measures to address the Black Cloud specifically and air pollution in general—such as promoting the use of natural gas as fuel for vehicles, factories and power plants and encouraging the recycling of rice straw instead of disposal through burning—the cloud still continues to appear and air pollution in general seems to be getting worse.

The reason for that is because the measures in place are insufficient and most lack proper enforcement.

A more holistic view of these measures and policies must be taken otherwise our environmental problems will continue to overshadow this country's future.

A Long-Term Policy Is Needed

Despite the fact that the current initiatives are heading in the right direction, they are merely the first installment of what needs to be done. A packaged policy framework that serves the goals of sustainable development is no longer an option, but a pressing necessity.

We need to look at problems related to the environment from a structural perspective. The government needs to be consistent with wanting to handle the pervasive environmental problems as part of achieving the overall well-being of Egyptians.

We need to start acting on the premise that economic growth cannot, and should not, overshadow environmental well-being.

With this in mind, economic, political and environmental policies all need to work in unison. This unfortunately is not the case as evident by the daily conflicts between what the government tries to achieve on the economic front and how that in turn affects environmental sustainability.

We need to start acting on the premise that economic growth cannot, and should not, overshadow environmental well-being. Even though the government subscribes to this view in rhetoric, we are yet to find a harmonized policy framework that serves to turn the goals of sustainable development into reality.

Short-Term Measures

While this is a long-term policy view that cannot be realized overnight, there are other measures that could instigate the short-term changes necessary for an overall change in the policy framework.

This will, however, involve environmental activism. If citizens stand up and voice their discontent with the current levels of air pollution in the capital, this may set in motion the wheel of policy change.

Short-term policy change would include added measures to address the levels of air pollution and more importantly, proper enforcement of those measures already in place. This will increase in the face of citizen pressure and the media attention that would ensue from environmental activism.

If the environmental activism that halted the Agrium plant in Damietta earlier this year [2008] was so effective, isn't it about time we saw such initiatives in the capital city?

Periodical and Internet Sources Bibliography

The following articles have been selected to supplement the diverse views presented in this chapter.

allAfrica.com	"Converting Vehicles to Gas to Fight Pollution," July 14, 2010.
Noah Dewitt	"Obroni Mail—Why No Emissions Standards?" *Accra Daily Mail* (Ghana), July 21, 2010.
Chiemelie Ezeobi	"Climate Change—The Women Step In," *This Day* (Nigeria), June 23, 2010.
Olga Gnativ	"What's Being Done to Burn Cleaner Car Fuel, Improve Air That Everyone Breathes," *Kyiv Post* (Ukraine), August 5, 2010.
Herald (Zimbabwe)	"Efforts to Reduce Air Pollution Intensified," February 24, 2010.
Dave Hill	"Not Clearing the Air," *Guardian* (UK), July 2, 2010.
Hindu (India)	"Care Air Centre Set Up to Monitor Emissions Online," June 22, 2010.
Matt Hodges	"Third Time Green for London," *China Daily*, July 27, 2010.
Isaac Khisa	"600 Armed Personnel to Protect Environment," *Monitor* (Uganda), June 7, 2010.
Paul Ogbuokiri	"Convention on Pollution from Ships Enters into Force," *Daily Champion* (Nigeria), July 8, 2010.
Michael Simire	"FG Signs Copenhagen Climate Accord," *Daily Independent* (Nigeria), June 27, 2010.

For Further Discussion

Chapter 1

1. After reading the viewpoints in this chapter, outline the hazardous effects of air pollution on health and the environment. From your reading, what countries seem to be having a serious problem with air pollution?

2. Andreas Lorenz discusses China's attempts to improve air quality before the Beijing Olympics. How bad was the air in Beijing? What were some of the challenges in getting an accurate picture of the true environmental situation in the city?

Chapter 2

1. How serious is the problem of indoor air pollution? In what part of the world is it a serious problem, and what causes it?

2. From your reading in this chapter, list some of the health problems associated with air pollution. How can countries address these problems?

Chapter 3

1. Two of the viewpoints in this chapter discuss the effects of Iceland's volcano and the recent Chinese sandstorms. What were the political and economical impacts of these two natural occurrences?

2. Jonathan Watts and Randeep Ramesh explore the political and economical challenges to improving environmental policy in the rapidly industrializing countries of India and China. Why is progress in this arena so slow and complicated?

Chapter 4

1. What clean air strategies examined in this chapter do you find the most efficient? Which do you believe has the most potential to improve air quality in your region?

2. In Stephen Harper's viewpoint, he talks about Alberta's state-of-the-art carbon capture and storage systems. What is carbon capture and storage? Do you think such systems are key in the fight to improve air quality?

Organizations to Contact

The editors have compiled the following list of organizations concerned with the issues debated in this book. The descriptions are derived from materials provided by the organizations. All have publications or information available for interested readers. The list was compiled on the date of publication of the present volume; the information provided here may change. Be aware that many organizations take several weeks or longer to respond to inquiries, so allow as much time as possible.

Air & Waste Management Association (A&WMA)
One Gateway Center, 3rd Floor, 420 Fort Duquesne Boulevard
Pittsburgh, PA   15222-1435
(800) 270-3444 • fax: (412) 232-3450
e-mail: info@awma.org
website: www.awma.org

The Air & Waste Management Association (A&WMA) is a nonprofit, nonpartisan professional organization that offers a forum for networking, information exchange, and public education for environmental professionals in sixty-five countries. A&WMA also strives to offer professional development opportunities for its members. It publishes the *Journal of the Air & Waste Management Association*, which features the latest in cutting-edge research and technology. Another publication, *EM*, covers the issues that impact today's environmental professionals.

Climate Action Network (CAN)
1810 Sixteenth Street NW, Washington, DC   20009
(202) 621-6309 • fax: (202) 536-5503
e-mail: info@climatenetwork.org
website: www.climatenetwork.org

The Climate Action Network (CAN) is a worldwide network of approximately five hundred nongovernmental organizations (NGOs) that work to limit human-induced climate change through individual action or government policies. These NGOs exchange information, network, and coordinate strategy on climate issues at every level. They also put together conferences, seminars, and other programs to bring members together to network and to find opportunities to work together. CAN publishes the *ECO* newsletters, which cover relevant environmental policy issues. On its website, CAN features a blog, video content, press releases, and video clips.

Environment Canada (EC)

351 St. Joseph Boulevard, Place Vincent Massey, 8th Floor
Gatineau, Quebec   K1A 0H3
(819) 997-2800 • fax: (819) 994-1412
e-mail: enviroinfo@ec.gc.ca
website: www.ec.gc.ca

Environment Canada (EC) is a Canadian government agency that strives to protect Canada's environment and to provide accurate weather and environmental predictions. EC's programs educate Canadians as to how to conserve their natural heritage and protect their surroundings. EC also coordinates the federal government's environmental policies and programs; conducts inspections; and initiates prosecutions of polluters and violators. EC publishes more than seven hundred peer-reviewed scientific publications, which are available on its website.

Environmental Defense Fund (EDF)

1875 Connecticut Avenue NW, Suite 600
Washington, DC   20009
(800) 684-3322 • fax: (212) 505-2375
website: www.edf.org

Established in 1967, the Environmental Defense Fund (EDF) is a nonprofit environmental advocacy group based in the United States that focuses on global warming, ecosystem restoration, clean oceans, and human health. Since it was founded by scientists, the EDF is committed to sound scientific research to address environmental problems. EDF has influenced public policy by recognizing global climate change as an urgent problem. The EDF website features blogs, podcasts, and commentary on the latest environmental issues as well as archives of *Solutions*, the EDF's quarterly newsletter.

Environmental Foundation for Africa (EFA)
1 Beach Road Lakka, Freetown Peninsula
PO Box PMB 34
  Sierra Leone
+232 76 684 832
e-mail: info@efsal.org.uk
website: www.efasl.org.uk

The Environmental Foundation for Africa (EFA) is a nongovernmental organization (NGO) based in Sierra Leone that works to protect and restore the natural environment in West Africa. Founded in 1992, the EFA creates educational programs and public campaigns to raise awareness about environmental issues, including the dangers of air pollution. It coordinates restoration and conservation projects; attempts to minimize the environmental damage done by civil wars and other conflicts; and lobbies for environmentally responsible practices and policies that will positively affect the lives of West African people as well as the natural environment. The EFA website features a photo gallery of some of the organization's work in Africa, information about recent and past EFA projects, and links to EFA annual reports and fact sheets.

European Environment Agency (EEA)
Kongens Nytorv 6, DK, Copenhagen K   1050
  Denmark
+45 33 36 71 00 • fax: +45 33 36 71 99
website: www.eea.europa.eu

The European Environment Agency (EEA) is the agency established by the European Union to monitor and protect Europe's natural environment. One of its main tasks is to "provide sound, independent information on the environment" and educate lawmakers, businesses, and European citizens on conservation practices and policies. The EEA also works to coordinate the European environment information and observation network. The EEA website has a range of video and animation on a variety of subjects; a full list of publications on environmental issues; statistics, maps, and graphs; and transcripts of speeches from EEA scientists and officials.

Institute for Energy Research (IER)

1100 H Street NW, Suite 400, Washington, DC   20005
(202) 621-2950 • fax: (202) 637-2420
website: www.instituteforenergyresearch.org

Founded in 1989, the Institute for Energy Research (IER) is a not-for-profit organization that conducts intensive research and analysis on the functions, operations, and government regulation of global energy markets. IER promotes the idea that unfettered energy markets provide the most efficient and effective solutions to today's global energy and environmental challenges and works to educate legislators, policy makers, and the public on the vital role offshore drilling plays in our energy future. IER publishes various fact sheets and comprehensive studies on renewable and nonrenewable energy sources, the growing green economy, climate change, and offshore oil exploration and drilling opportunities. IER also maintains a blog on its website, which provides timely comment on relevant energy and legislative issues.

International Energy Agency

9 rue de la Fédération, Paris Cedex 15   75739
   France
+33 1 40 57 65 00 • fax: +33 1 40 57 65 09
e-mail: info@iea.org
website: www.iea.org

The International Energy Agency (IEA) is an intergovernmental association that advises its twenty-eight member countries on issues of energy policy and clean energy. The IEA focuses on finding solutions for its members on energy security, economic development, and environmental protection, especially regarding climate change. It conducts energy research and statistical compilation to assess the current state of the energy market and future trends in the industry; disseminates the latest energy news and policy analyses; and provides well-researched recommendations to member states. The agency publishes numerous in-depth reports offering insight on the energy industry and specific energy topics as well as its monthly newsletter, *IEA Open Energy Technology Bulletin*, which provides regular updates on energy security and environmental issues.

Union of Concerned Scientists (UCS)

2 Brattle Square, Cambridge, MA   02138-3780
(617) 547-5552 • fax: (617) 864-9405
website: www.ucsusa.org

Founded by scientists and students at the Massachusetts Institute of Technology in 1969, the Union of Concerned Scientists (UCS) is a science-based, nonprofit organization working for a healthy environment and a safer world. UCS utilizes independent scientific research and citizen action "to develop innovative, practical solutions and to secure responsible changes in government policy, corporate practices, and consumer choices." UCS publishes in-depth reports on several important issues: global warming, scientific integrity, clean energy and vehicles, global security, and food and agriculture. It also publishes the *Catalyst* magazine, *Earthwise* newsletter, and *Greentips Newsletter*.

United Nations Environment Programme (UNEP)

United Nations Avenue, Gigiri, PO Box 30552
Nairobi   00100
   Kenya
(254-20) 7621234 • fax: (254-20) 7624489
e-mail: unepinfo@unep.org
website: www.unep.org

The United Nations Environment Programme (UNEP) is an agency that advocates for and provides support to developing countries that are working to implement environmentally sound policies and practices. The UNEP strives "to provide leadership and encourage partnership in caring for the environment by inspiring, informing, and enabling nations and peoples to improve their quality of life without compromising that of future generations." The UNEP website features animation, videos, podcasts, photos, and a UNEP TV station that focus on environmental issues all over the world and provide information on UNEP programs and activities. It also lists UNEP studies, periodicals, and books as well as links to UNEP newsletters on subjects as varied as the Great Apes Survival Project and sustainable consumption. There is also an e-calendar of events, including conventions and special days like World Water Day.

US Energy Association (USEA)

1300 Pennsylvania Avenue NW, Suite 550, Mailbox 142
Washington, DC   20004-3022
(202) 312-1230 • fax: (202) 682-1682
e-mail: reply@usea.org
website: www.usea.org

The United States Energy Association (USEA) is an association of public and private energy-related organizations, corporations, and government agencies. It promotes the varied interests of the US energy sector by disseminating information to increase the understanding of energy issues. In conjunction with the US Agency for International Development and the US Department of Energy, USEA sponsors the Energy Partnership Program as well as numerous policy reports and conferences dealing with global and domestic energy issues. USEA also organizes trade and educational exchange visits with other countries. Reports and other publications, speeches, and presentations can be found on its website.

US Environmental Protection Agency (EPA)
Ariel Rios Building, 1200 Pennsylvania Avenue NW
Washington, DC   20460
(202) 272-0167
website: www.epa.gov

The Environmental Protection Agency (EPA) is a US governmental agency that is tasked with protecting America's natural environment and safeguarding human health. The key responsibility of the EPA is to write and enforce environmental regulations. Established in 1970, the agency also conducts environmental research, provides assessments on environmental problems, and offers education on environmental policy and practices. The EPA works closely with local, state, and tribal governments to offer feedback and guidance on environmental policies and problems. The EPA website offers a monthly newsletter, *Go Green!*; a listing of environmental laws and regulations; updates on recent programs and initiatives; transcripts of speeches, seminars, and testimony; and in-depth research on environmental issues.

Bibliography of Books

Braden Allenby   *Reconstructing Earth: Technology and Environment in the Age of Humans.* Washington, DC: Island Press, 2005.

Jon Ayres, Robert Maynard, and Roy Richards, eds.   *Air Pollution and Health.* London: Imperial College Press, 2006.

Gilbert M. Bankobeza   *Ozone Protection: The International Legal Regime.* Utrecht, the Netherlands: Eleven International Publishing, 2005.

Virginia Warner Brodine   *Red Roots, Green Shoots.* Edited by Marc Brodine. New York: International Publishers, 2007.

Julie Kerr Casper   *Greenhouse Gases: Worldwide Impacts.* New York: Facts on File, 2010.

Hugh Compston and Ian Bailey, eds.   *Turning Down the Heat: The Politics of Climate Policy in Affluent Democracies.* New York: Palgrave Macmillan, 2008.

Peter Dauvergne   *The Shadows of Consumption: Consequences for the Global Environment.* Cambridge, MA: MIT Press, 2008.

John S. Dryzek   *The Politics of the Earth: Environmental Discourses.* New York: Oxford University Press, 2005.

Douglas S. Eisinger   *Smog Check: Science, Federalism, and the Politics of Clean Air.* Washington, DC: RFF Press, 2010.

John Bellamy Foster	*The Ecological Revolution: Making Peace with the Planet.* New York: Monthly Review Press, 2009.
Alexander Y. Galashev	*Climatic Effects Created by Atmospheric Greenhouse Gases.* Hauppauge, NY: Nova Science, 2011.
Alexander Gillespie	*Climate Change, Ozone Depletion and Air Pollution.* Boston, MA: M. Nijhoff, 2006.
George A. Gonzalez	*The Politics of Air Pollution: Urban Growth, Ecological Modernization, and Symbolic Inclusion.* Albany: State University of New York Press, 2005.
Bhola R. Gurjar, Luisa T. Molina, and C.S.P. Ojha, eds.	*Air Pollution: Health and Environmental Impacts.* Boca Raton, FL: Taylor & Francis, 2010.
Clive Hamilton	*Scorcher: The Dirty Politics of Climate Change.* Melbourne: Black Inc. Agenda, 2007.
Jonathan Harrington	*The Climate Diet: How You Can Cut Carbon, Cut Costs, and Save the Planet.* London: EarthScan, 2008.
Martin Keogh, ed.	*Hope Beneath Our Feet: Restoring Our Place in the Natural World.* Berkeley, CA: North Atlantic Books, 2010.
Anthony S. Kessel	*Air, the Environment, and Public Health.* Cambridge, UK: Cambridge University Press, 2006.

Sonia Labatt and
Rodney R. White

Carbon Finance: The Financial Implications of Climate Change. Hoboken, NJ: John Wiley & Sons, 2007.

W. Henry
Lambright

NASA and the Environment: The Case of Ozone Depletion. Washington, DC: NASA, 2005.

Patrick J.
Michaels, ed.

Shattered Consensus: The True State of Global Warming. Lanham, MD: Rowman & Littlefield, 2005.

Karen T.
Morningstar, ed.

Carbon Offsets: Examining Their Role in Greenhouse Gas Reduction. New York: Nova Science Publishers, 2010.

Stephen A.
Rackley

Carbon Capture and Storage. Burlington, MA: Butterworth-Heinemann, 2010.

Simon Shackley
and Clair Gough,
eds.

Carbon Capture and Its Storage: An Integrated Assessment. Aldershot, England: Ashgate, 2006.

Richard C.J.
Somerville

The Forgiving Air: Understanding Environmental Change. 2nd ed. Boston, MA: American Meteorological Society, 2008.

T.H. Tietenberg

Emissions Trading: Principles and Practice. 2nd ed. Washington, DC: Resources for the Future, 2006.

Steve
Vanderheiden

Atmospheric Justice: A Political Theory of Climate Change. New York: Oxford University Press, 2008.

Index

Geographic headings and page numbers in **boldface** refer to viewpoints about that country or region.